a legacy of
Health & Healing

Stories of Early Adventist Health Care

Jane Allen Quevedo

Foreword by Mardian J. Blair

Copyright © 2016 Jane Allen Quevado

Copyright © 2016 Teach Services, Inc.

ISBN-13: 978-1-47960-718-1

Library of Congress Control Number: 2016913208

TEACH Services, Inc.
P U B L I S H I N G
www.TEACHServices.com ● (800) 367-1844

ACKNOWLEDGEMENTS

For his vision to produce this collection of stories, his wise counsel and overall direction of the project, and his commitment to see it finished

Mardian J. Blair

For their careful review of the manuscript and helpful suggestions

Wally Coe, Pat Benton, Frank Dupper, William Murrill,
Ray and Virginia Pelton, Benjamin Reaves, Don and Doris Roth,
Royce and Elaine Thompson, Rita Waterman,
and many, many others

For sharing their experiences, letters, tapes, and other documents

Dozens of kind and helpful people around the world

For the corporate sponsorship that made the original book possible,
A Thousand Miracles Every Day, as well as this abridged version,
A Legacy of Health and Healing: Stories of Early Adventist Health Care

ADVENTIST HEALTH SYSTEM
900 Hope Way
Altamonte Springs, Florida 32714

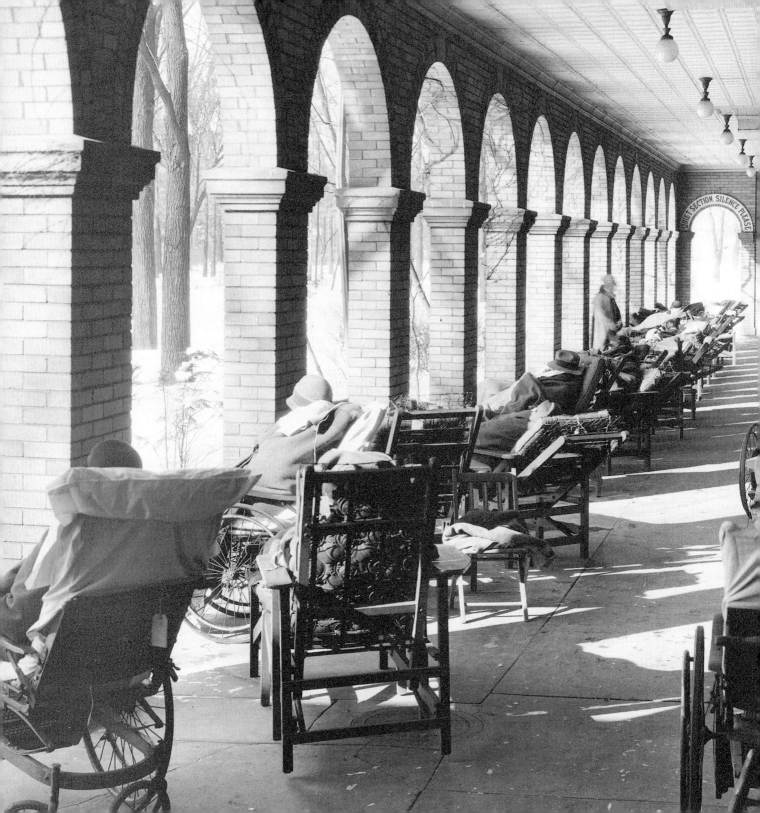

CONTENTS

Foreword iv

Introduction vi

Battle Creek Sanitarium 1

St. Helena Hospital 9

Boulder Memorial Hospital 17

Portland Adventist Medical Center 21

Walla Walla General Hospital 27

Paradise Valley Hospital 33

Glendale Adventist Medical Center 41

Loma Linda University Health 49

Adventist Medical Center Hinsdale 59

Washington Adventist Hospital 71

Tennessee Christian Medical Center 79

Florida Hospital 87

Park Ridge Health 95

White Memorial Medical Center 101

Takoma Regional Hospital 109

Porter Adventist Hospital 117

Florida Hospital Heartland Medical Center 125

Feather River Hospital 131

Sonora Community Hospital 141

Battle Creek Health Center 147

Shawnee Mission Medical Center 153

Castle Medical Center 159

Kettering Medical Center 163

Manchester Memorial Hospital 173

Texas Health Huguley Hospital 183

Appendix A 188

Appendix B – Chronology 192

FOREWORD

In early 1999 I addressed a group of health care and church leaders at a Conference on Mission sponsored by Adventist Health System in Orlando, Florida. It was my final presentation to this group prior to my retirement as its president, and I shared some stories I learned during my career in Adventist health care. These narratives played an important part in my own education as a young health care executive in the Seventh-day Adventist Church. They taught me much about the history and culture of the organization to which I would devote my professional life.

I shared about my boss, A.C. Larson at Hinsdale Hospital, and how our conversations often turned to the early days of Adventist hospitals. Examples include the story of the Denver businessman who received a 45-cent refund and later built the Porter Sanitarium (Porter Adventist Hospital) and the account of how Dr. David Paulson repeatedly received unexpected money, at the exact time needed to sustain Hinsdale Sanitarium (Adventist Medical Center Hinsdale).

Most of the people in my audience that day had never heard these stories, and their positive comments afterward seemed to be more than just polite courtesies. It was then that I realized the enormous value of publishing a single volume of collected stories related to the history, development, and culture of Adventist hospitals. Such a collection could serve as a resource not only for leaders, but also for church members, employees, physicians, students, and many others.

What you are holding is an abridged version of that original book—*A Thousand Miracles Every Day*—researched and written by Jane Allen Quevedo, communication director at Adventist Health System from 1985 to 1995. With her permission and oversight, this reprint was edited and updated by Adventist Health System for publication in 2016 to coincide with the 150th anniversary celebration of Adventist health care. It begins with a brief review of the Battle Creek story, which establishes a background for the stories that follow. For this reprint, we limited coverage to hospitals established prior to 1980, which are still in operation today, with a few exceptions due to history and affiliation. In addition, the stories and personalities highlighted are limited to those featured when the book was originally published in 2003. While many individuals have served and contributed to Adventist health care since that time, their stories are not included in this edition.

Our search for information took many routes, including Adventist Yearbooks and encyclopedias, as well as other books, brochures, articles, letters, documents, unpublished manuscripts, tape recordings, and personal interviews. These primary sources are listed at the end of each chapter. No attempt was made to treat all hospitals equally. The objective was to gather human-interest stories and present them within the context of each hospital's story.

Over the years, thousands of men and women helped develop Adventist health care around the world. In spite of hardships, these pioneers remained steadfast in their mission. Some sold their homes to build a hospital. They took on personal debt and worked long hours, sometimes without pay. Some gave up personal ambitions and lucrative positions to serve in places where success depended upon their own ingenuity and the grace of God.

When organizations lose sight of their roots, they risk drifting from their purpose. With time, the early accounts of sacrifice become lost, forgotten, or so changed that they bear little resemblance to the actual experience. We hope this book helps to preserve the stories, not only reflecting the heritage of Adventist health care, but most importantly, God's blessing and providential leading in the growth of these health care organizations and the lives of those extending care, as the human expression of the healing ministry of Christ.

Mardian J. Blair
President Emeritus
Adventist Health System
1984 - 2000

INTRODUCTION

The Battle Creek story represents the first chapter in the history of Adventist health care. The Seventh-day Adventist Church had already established its headquarters and a publishing house in Battle Creek when it opened the Western Health Reform Institute in 1866, and soon afterward it would open Battle Creek College.

These organizations produced many nurses and other medical missionaries who could teach, preach, and give simple health treatments. Wherever they went, the Adventists from Battle Creek took health care with them—lecturing at evangelistic meetings, operating treatment rooms and sanitariums, or dispensing medicines at overseas mission stations. For a short time the church even operated a medical school at Battle Creek, graduating several physicians who helped establish some of the facilities that are the anchors of Adventist health care today.

As a result of this early activity, nearly 20 of today's Adventist hospitals opened their doors between 1866 and 1913, including St. Helena Hospital, Portland Adventist Medical Center, Walla Walla General Hospital, Glendale Adventist Medical Center, Loma Linda University Health, Adventist Medical Center Hinsdale, Washington Adventist Hospital, Florida Hospital, Park Ridge Health, and White Memorial Medical Center.

The next expansion occurred outside the United States. While early missionaries had operated treatment rooms and dispensaries and even established overseas sanitariums, the years between 1915 and 1945 saw a tremendous increase in the number of overseas facilities. These early ventures included Sydney Adventist Hospital, River Plate Sanitarium and Hospital, Malamulo Hospital, Lake Geneva Sanitarium, and Simla Sanitarium and Hospital. In the U.S., only two Adventist hospitals in operation today were established during this time—Takoma Regional Hospital in 1928, and Porter Adventist Hospital in 1930.

The end of World War II ushered in the era of the Adventist community hospital. New medicines and technologies, insurance plans, Medicare, and other advances changed health care forever. Sanitarium programs featuring lectures, recreation, and extended "vacations" soon became history. The early health centers shed the "sanitarium" part of their names as their business shifted to acute care.

By this time Adventists were known for operating a special kind of hospital where caregivers offered extraordinary care that emphasized the importance of treating the whole person. Communities across the United States invited the church to help them build and operate their hospitals. As medical science brought technological advances and capabilities, Adventist hospitals added programs and services to meet the needs and expectations of the ever-increasing number of people they served. Eventually, tertiary-care hospitals greatly expanded the church's health care ministry in terms of quality and service.

Today, there are five Adventist health care systems in the United States: Loma Linda University Health, Kettering Health Network, Adventist Health, Adventist HealthCare and Adventist Health System.

A Legacy of Health and Healing: Stories of Early Adventist Health Care chronicles the vision, sacrifice, dedication, and overriding hand of divine providence in the development of Adventist hospitals from the late 1800s to the beginning of the 21st century. Adventist health care has united Adventists in a common mission and strengthened their ministry in those communities. As a ministry, Adventist health care must always recognize its place in God's plan to extend the healing ministry of Christ to those who are sick and hurting. In this context it continues to be a story of miracles— more than a thousand every day.

To learn more, visit: SDAHealthCare.org | AdventistHealthSystem.com

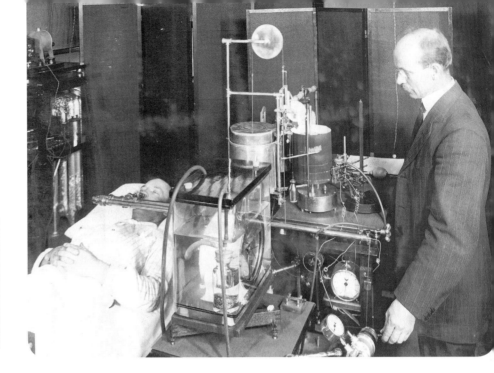

Vision, Verandahs, and Divine Providence

Battle Creek Sanitarium: Battle Creek, Michigan | 1866–1933

Every Adventist health care organization traces its heritage to Battle Creek, Michigan, where the young Seventh-day Adventist Church established the Western Health Reform Institute in 1866. Typically, the history of an early Adventist hospital begins with a description of a Victorian structure surrounded by broad verandahs and spacious lawns where guests relaxed and enjoyed outdoor activities in the fresh air and sunshine. A collection of photographs might show patients arriving at a sanitarium in a horse-drawn buggy, nurses in white starched uniforms giving hydrotherapy treatments, and stern-faced physicians posing next to the latest medical invention of the early 1900s. The narrative describing early days at "The San" likely discusses the visionary leadership of Ellen G. White and the innovative Dr. John Harvey Kellogg, who devoted 68 years of his life to helping people live healthfully.

Ellen G. White...promoted a rational approach to health, emphasizing exercise, rest, wholesome diet, fresh air, sunshine, water, abstinence from harmful substances, and trust in God.

At the height of its popularity, the world-famous Battle Creek Sanitarium attracted the likes of Henry Ford, Thomas Edison, J.C. Penney, Clara Barton, George Bernard Shaw, John D. Rockefeller, Jr., Dale Carnegie, and Amelia Earhart. They and hundreds of others came to Battle Creek to recuperate from the stress and unhealthy choices of their busy lives. Here they would get hydrotherapy treatments and massages, participate in recreational and exercise activities, and dine on sometimes-experimental dishes designed for the most health-conscious.

Certainly, one of the sanitarium's biggest attractions was its medical director, Dr. John Harvey Kellogg, a skillful surgeon, advocate of vegetarianism, and proponent of the natural laws of health. Kellogg joined the Western Health Reform Institute about nine years after it opened, renamed it Battle Creek Medical and Surgical Sanitarium, and developed it into a world-famous center. At its prime in the 1920s, it could accommodate 1,500 guests.

The Battle Creek Sanitarium was founded on the concept that health care was vital to the Seventh-day Adventist mission to relieve human suffering. Ellen G. White, author, speaker, and visionary accepted by the church as divinely inspired, believed in the interrelationship of physical, mental, and spiritual well-being. She promoted a rational approach to health, emphasizing exercise, rest, wholesome diet, fresh air, sunshine, water, abstinence from harmful substances, and trust in God. Ellen's husband, James White, had suffered from ill health due largely to overwork and a poor diet. He went to a New York facility specializing in water treatments. While

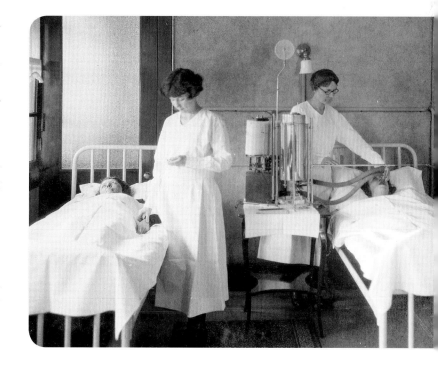

making some improvement, he did not fully recover until he returned home, changed his diet and followed his wife's advice to add some physical and mental activity to his daily program. White's experience gave added impetus to his wife's counsel that the Seventh-day Adventist Church should establish a health ministry as "the right arm" of its gospel ministry.

While Mrs. White and Dr. Kellogg were key figures in the history of the Battle Creek Sanitarium, another White and Kellogg figured prominently in the pioneer effort, too. James White and the doctor's father, J. P. Kellogg, were among those who bought company stocks to begin the institute. Kellogg, father of 11 children, operated a broom factory, and for many years he generously supported the fledgling church.

James White supported the health center from the beginning. In the early days, when it appeared that it would not succeed, he stepped in to help rescue it from failure. Under White's administration, the institute's sagging bottom line began to improve. However, qualified physicians were needed. Over the years the Whites had watched the Kellogg children grow up and were especially taken with young John Harvey. They encouraged him to study medicine and return to Battle Creek and even paid some of his school expenses. Kellogg studied at the Trall's Hygieo-Therapeutic College in New Jersey, the University of Michigan, and Bellevue Hospital Medical College in New York. He returned to Battle Creek and at age 24 was appointed medical superintendent.

Kellogg was an energetic, enthusiastic, inventive, and persuasive personality with big ideas. Traveling around the world, he preached the gospel of health and promoted his ideas on "biologic living." He invented, among other things, peanut butter, cornflakes, exercise equipment, and even a mechanical horse for President Calvin Coolidge.

He studied surgery in Europe under some of the world's leading physicians. It is reported that he performed more than 22,000 operations. Dr. Dunbar Smith, who served at the Battle Creek hospital in the 1950s, had the opportunity to examine some of Kellogg's patients and found the surgery scars to be barely visible.

At the height of its popularity, the world-famous Battle Creek Sanitarium attracted the likes of Henry Ford, Thomas Edison, J.C. Penney, Clara Barton, George Bernard Shaw, John D. Rockefeller, Jr., Dale Carnegie, and Amelia Earhart.

The need for qualified physicians continued to be a problem. To help alleviate the situation, promising students were selected to pursue medicine at secular universities. Often, however, they returned to Battle Creek with ideas that didn't fit squarely with the philosophy of the sanitarium. Around 1891 a plan was developed for students to share a home in Ann Arbor while studying at the University of Michigan. This provided them with a Christian environment while they pursued their studies.

The class included David Paulson, future founder of Hinsdale Hospital near Chicago; Edgar Caro, future medical director of the forerunner of Sydney Adventist Hospital in Australia; and Daniel and Lauretta Kress, who later served in England, Australia, New Zealand, and at Washington Adventist Hospital in Takoma Park, Maryland.

Unsatisfied with the way prospective doctors were being educated, the Battle Creek Sanitarium board voted to begin a medical school under Kellogg's leadership. American Medical Missionary

College opened in 1895, with the main campus in Battle Creek and the clinical division in Chicago, both directed by Paulson.

The medical school, free clinics, and other expansion efforts severely drained the denomination's finances. Church leaders preferred to keep the sanitarium small, adding other facilities as opportunities arose and money became available. Kellogg and the church came to disagree over this approach, as well as over other issues such as admission policies to the medical school, points of doctrine, and ultimately ownership of the sanitarium. Among the biggest controversies was the rebuilding of the facility after fire destroyed it in 1902.

Kellogg ignored the counsel he had been given to construct a single building, not more than five stories high and 450 feet in length. Instead, he built a huge structure featuring marble pillars and five acres of marble mosaic floors—reported to be the best-equipped facility of its kind in the world.

Unable to work with Kellogg and wishing to avoid centralization of their work, church leaders focused their attention elsewhere. In 1903 they moved their headquarters to Washington, D.C. and began looking for a place for a medical school. Finding a number of failed health care facilities and resorts at bargain prices in Southern California, they purchased one near San Bernardino called Loma Linda. In 1906 they opened a school, which would become the College of Medical Evangelists, today's Loma Linda University. Many members of the staff and faculty joined the California school.

Enrollment at American Medical Missionary College declined, and the school closed in 1910. Kellogg operated the Battle Creek Sanitarium until his death in 1943. While he and the church never officially reconciled, Kellogg and the Battle Creek Sanitarium played important roles in establishing the medical work of the Seventh-day Adventist Church. As the following pages reveal, their influence was felt for many years in hospitals, dispensaries, clinics, and treatment rooms all around the world.

THE DAILY GRAND MARCH, BATTLE CREEK SANITARIUM, BATTLE CREEK, MICHIGAN

SOURCES

Robinson, D.E. *The Story of Our Health Message*, Nashville, Tennessee: Southern Publishing Association, 1956.

Schaefer, Richard A., *Legacy: Daring to Care*, Loma Linda, California: Legacy Publishing Association, 1995.

Schwarz, Richard W., *John Harvey Kellogg, M.D.*, Nashville, Tennessee: Southern Publishing Association, 1970.

Smith, Dunbar W., M.D., *The Travels, Triumphs and Vicissitudes of Dunbar W. Smith, M.D.*, Loma Linda: Dunbar W. Smith, M.D., 1994.

Where Adventist Health Care Began in the West

St. Helena Hospital: Deer Park, California | Founded 1878

Before the first Adventist health center opened in Battle Creek, or the first Seventh-day Adventist missionary sailed the Atlantic, or John Harvey Kellogg entered medical school, Merritt Gardner Kellogg trekked across the United States in an oxcart. Arriving in San Francisco in 1859, the eldest Kellogg brother and his family are thought to be the first Seventh-day Adventists in California.

Kellogg worked as a carpenter to pay the bills, but his real passions were sharing his faith and establishing church congregations. Believing that his work in California would be more effective if he had some medical training, Kellogg moved to New Jersey in 1867 and enrolled at Trall's Hygieo-Therapeutic College. There he completed a six-month medical course, which in those days qualified him to use the title "Doctor."

Before returning to the West Coast, he persuaded two Adventist ministers to join him, J.N. Loughborough and D.T. Bourdeau. These three worked together for some time, with the ministers preaching the gospel and the doctor giving health lectures. When a smallpox epidemic broke out near Santa Rosa in 1870, Kellogg and Loughborough stopped their public meetings to care for the sick. People were impressed by the doctor's successful treatment with water therapy and a healthy diet. About 10 of every 11 patients recovered under his care, compared to only one in five by another physician using popular drug treatments of the day.

Soon others joined Kellogg in California. By the mid-1870s, Adventists in the state numbered around 500, and their number grew steadily. Loughborough, president of the newly organized California Conference of Seventh-day Adventists, had helped establish the Battle Creek Sanitarium, and he hoped someday to start a similar facility in Northern California. In 1874, he and one of his associates, I.D. Van Horn, were in St. Helena looking for potential church sites when Van Horn found an attractive hillside property overlooking a valley. It had a spring, and he thought it was an ideal place for a health center. The property belonged to William Pratt, a retired bricklayer and recent convert to the Adventist faith.

However, nothing happened with that idea until sometime later. Kellogg had settled in Napa Valley, a few miles south of St. Helena, and continued his medical practice there while working closely with the ministers. The doctor and a patient's husband, A.B. Atwood, talked of the need for a medical facility, and soon they were making plans. Atwood came up with $1,000, Kellogg gave $1,000 in labor, and Pratt donated 10 acres of his hillside property.

Others came along beside them to make the hospital a reality. Among the early stockholders was John Morrison of Santa Rosa, who received $200 worth of stock in exchange for a team of horses used to haul lumber. Construction of a two-story frame building began in 1878 using bricks made of clay from the local hillsides and baked in kilns in Pratt's yard.

In the church magazine *Signs of the Times* (November 22, 1877), Kellogg proclaimed, "The location is all that could be desired…. The climate, location, and surroundings are not second to any other locality in California for the recovery and preservation of health."

The 13-bed Rural Health Retreat in St. Helena opened in June, 1878. Ellen G. White spoke at the dedication, declaring, "…the very surroundings exert an influence in calling us to higher and purer lives." Within a week, every bed was occupied, and tents were pitched in the yard to house employees and patient overflow. In fact, some early guests preferred to stay in tents to fully enjoy the mountain air.

John Burden, another significant figure in early Adventist health care, joined St. Helena Sanitarium as business manager in 1891. At that time the facility was reportedly the largest of its kind on the West Coast. It even had branches in San Francisco, Sacramento, and Eureka, California, as well as Honolulu. (Burden went on to help develop three other major Adventist health care facilities in Southern California—Paradise Valley, Glendale, and Loma Linda—as well as the Sydney Sanitarium in Australia.)

St. Helena Sanitarium (renamed in 1890) opened one of the first schools of nursing in California and was the first to graduate a male nurse. Interestingly, male nurses in those days did not perform such bedside tasks as taking a patient's temperature and pulse. The men chopped wood, delivered specimen jars, and set up cots for the night shift. According to 1928 graduate Olin Bray, male nurses gave hydrotherapy treatments during the day and were assigned "cot duty" with alcoholic and psychiatric patients at night.

While studies and work occupied much of their time, the male student nurses found time for some enterprising ventures, such as making their own root beer. Former hospital staff member Pat Benton reported, "They filled disposable glass intravenous flasks with their 'brew' and frequently shared it with the girls. Root beer floats concocted from the boys' stock and cafeteria ice cream were a favorite for many years."

The thriving health retreat spawned a little community known as Sanitarium, with a post office that opened in 1901. In the aftermath of the 1906 San Francisco earthquake, many fled to this mountain community. Again tents were put to good use as temporary housing.

A historical transcript describing life at the St. Helena Sanitarium in 1939 offers a glimpse into Adventist health centers in the 1930s and 1940s. While the facility provided acute-care medical, surgical, and maternity services, it also offered the traditional sanitarium programs featuring hydrotherapy, massage, nutrition, physical and occupational therapy, and other preventative medicine programs. At St. Helena, the sanitarium section was completely separate from the acute-care facility.

Sanitarium guests arriving by car were met by pages who escorted them across the verandah and inside to the registration desk. A hand-operated elevator transported guests upstairs to the comfortably furnished rooms, some with writing desks and vanities for patient convenience. Most likely the rooms were decorated with fresh flowers because employees would gather wildflowers from the Napa Valley, while guests picked flowers from the sanitarium gardens where they usually worked.

Each day began with reveille and the raising of the flag at sunrise. Guests were expected to be on the roof at 7 a.m., where a physical therapist led them in morning exercises—complete with live piano accompaniment. Other activities included croquet, tennis, archery, and darts. An intercom system throughout the hospital kept patients informed of various events throughout the day, such as the evening parlor program or twice-a-day band concerts performed by hospital employees.

If they were well enough, guests ate their meals in the dining room, along with staff members and visitors from all over California's North Bay Area. A dining room hostess seated the

Each day began with reveille and the raising of the flag at sunrise. Guests were expected to be on the roof at 7 a.m., where a physical therapist led them in morning exercises—complete with live piano accompaniment.

guests, who selected their meals from a menu and were served by waiters. St. Helena Sanitarium and Hospital served vegetarian food exclusively from 1915 until 1984. The collection of birds, fish, and deer on the hospital campus were strictly for the guests' visual enjoyment and never appeared on their dinner plates. The hospital's physical building developed over the years as health care changed and the staff endeavored to meet patient needs. The original structure was replaced in 1968. Shortly thereafter, St. Helena Hospital faced one of the most critical times in its history, and by the early 1970s was in danger of closing. Looking for a way to turn around its finances and meet the community's needs, St. Helena took a bold step by starting a cardiology program, including open-heart surgery.

A group of physicians pooled funds in 1972 to equip a cardiovascular catheterization lab, making St. Helena Hospital the first in California's North Bay Area to perform coronary angiograms. Dr. Charles Tam would fly from Southern California on Sundays to perform angiograms with Dr. Wilson White. Tam and his physician brother, Wilfred, eventually moved to St. Helena in 1974. Working with White, they created the first cardiac surgery team and program in the area. Before emergency coronary angiograms and coronary artery bypass procedures were even options at most hospitals, these innovations had become standard treatments for heart attacks at St. Helena Hospital.

The world's oldest continuously operating Adventist health center has continued to expand its services to address the health needs in Northern California through its acute care and comprehensive hospital-based wellness programs. In addition, nearly 140 years after the St. Helena Hospital was founded, this tranquil, private setting overlooking the Napa Valley remains a perfect backdrop for learning the principles of healthful living. While it faced some big challenges in its long history, the hospital successfully weathered the storms of change and remains faithful to its mission of sharing God's love.

In the church magazine *Signs of the Times* (November 22, 1877), Kellogg proclaimed, "The location is all that could be desired.... The climate, location, and surroundings are not second to any other locality in California for the recovery and preservation of health."

SOURCES

"A Century of Progress 1878-1978: St. Helena Hospital and Health Center Celebrates 100 Years," 1978.

Benton, Pat, "From Hydrotherapy to Heart Surgery," *Pacific Union Recorder*, August 5, 1991.

Johns, Warren L., and Richard H. Utt, editors, *The Vision Bold*, Washington, D.C.: Review and Herald Publishing Association, 1977.

"St. Helena Sanitarium and Hospital: Established 1878," undated.

"Sanitarium Dedication, Open House Sunday," *St. Helena Star*, May 9, 1968.

"Transcription of Historical Tape," undated.

"Where the Ministry of Healing Takes Place," Pacific Union Recorder, June 6, 1978.

Interview: Erwin Remboldt.

Colorado Mountain Resort

Boulder Memorial Hospital: Boulder, Colorado | 1893–1989

The gold rush of 1858 and 1859 enticed thousands of fortune-seekers to Colorado, but the real population boom came several decades later with the flood of tuberculosis patients known as "lungers." By the 1920s, more than half of Denver's population was attributed to the TB treatment facilities. In nearby Boulder, Adventists had opened the Colorado Sanitarium in 1893 after a retired minister had visited the area and persuaded Dr. John Harvey Kellogg to start a health program there. Dr. Robert Horner, whose grandfather was a patient at the Colorado Sanitarium, recalled:

> *My grandfather arrived in Denver in the late 1890s looking for a tuberculosis cure. He did not have the name or address of a TB facility, but his neighbors in North Dakota had told him there was one in Colorado. So, he bought a train ticket and figured he would find the place after he got there. As soon as he arrived, he started asking, "Where do the 'lungers' go?"*
>
> *"Take the train to Boulder," one man told him. "The 'Advents' have built a place right up against the mountains, and they will take good care of you."*
>
> *After about two months of sunshine, exercise, improved diet, plenty of water, and hydrotherapy treatments at the Colorado Sanitarium, Granddad was well on his way to recovery. However, he had no money to pay his bill of about one dollar a day. The sanitarium allowed him to pay off the debt by working as an elevator operator.*

The cool mountain setting of the Boulder-Colorado Sanitarium, as it was named in 1905, attracted people wishing to escape the steamy summer weather of Texas and other southern states. For outdoor recreation, they enjoyed horseback riding and mountain climbing, as well as nature walks. The Boulder facility followed the blueprint of other early Adventist sanitariums, offering scientific medical care while promoting the concepts of wellness and natural healing.

Dr. Kate Lindsay was among the first physicians on the sanitarium's medical staff, and she served there for about 20 years. However, H.A. Green, director of the facility from 1910 to 1937, is the physician most closely identified with the early days of the Boulder San. In fact, for many years it was known as "Dr. Green's Sanitarium." It was renamed Boulder Memorial Hospital in 1962.

Dramatic changes came to all Adventist health care facilities as the sanitarium era gave way to the age of acute-care hospitals. The Boulder hospital bridged the old with the new by building upon its long-established hydrotherapy program. It developed a physical medicine and rehabilitation department that ranked among the best in Colorado.

However, with a changing marketplace, increased competition, and resulting financial losses, the Boulder facility was sold in 1989. A new 50-bed facility called Avista Adventist Hospital opened in 1990 in the growing community of Louisville, about six miles from Boulder. Louisville is a thriving young community near the University of Colorado and home to several high-tech industries.

"Where do the 'lungers' go?" "Take the train to Boulder," one man told him. "The 'Advents' have built a place right up against the mountains, and they will take good care of you."

SOURCES

Briggs, Bill, "Denver Stands Tall Among Healthiest Cities," *Denver Post*, April 15, 2001.

Interviews and Notes: Dr. Robert Horner and Ron Sackett.

Northwest Pioneers

Portland Adventist Medical Center: Portland, Oregon | Founded 1893

Dr. Louis Belknap was robbed while traveling through San Francisco and arrived in Portland, Oregon, nearly penniless. A student of Dr. John Harvey Kellogg, Belknap had traveled from Battle Creek to the "Wild West" in 1893 to begin a health care venture. Although Adventists had established churches in Oregon as early as the 1870s, they had not launched any medical work.

Pastor T.H. Starbuck loaned the doctor some money to get his work started. Belknap rented an eight-room house and set up a six-bed "sanitarium for nervous diseases" that specialized in hydrotherapy and water cure treatments. With financial help from local church members, in 1895 Belknap went on to set up the Portland Sanitarium in the Reed Mansion, a large ornate house with room for 20 patients, a surgical ward, an office, a kitchen, and a dining room. The house included a stable that was remodeled to serve as treatment rooms and a nurses' dormitory.

The Belknaps left Oregon for California in 1896, and the Adventist church, through the International Medical Missionary and Benevolent Association, took over the sanitarium. After adding a two-year nurses' training program and the Portland Sanitarium Health Food Company in 1897, the Portland San quickly became the church's flagship facility in the Northwest.

> "The nurses and other staff have created a unique difference because of the continued emphasis on spiritual care for years and years."
>
> – LARRY DODDS

By 1902 the sanitarium had outgrown the Reed Mansion. Several acres were purchased on Mt. Tabor, where a four-story, 75-bed facility was built for $50,000. This bright red, wooden structure with broad verandahs could be seen easily against the green hillside. With no improved roads leading to the site, a steam train from Portland brought patients to within a few blocks of the San.

Dr. William Holden, a highly regarded physician and surgeon, joined the medical staff in 1903. His surgical skills attracted patients and helped the hospital to grow into a modern medical center. By 1919 surgery represented about half of the sanitarium's business.

Holden and members of his family served continuously on Portland's medical staff since 1903. Holden was on staff until his death in 1955, serving as medical director from 1910 to 1920, and again from 1924 to 1943, for a total of 29 years. Dr. William Rippy, Holden's son-in-law, later served on the staff, followed by a grandson, Dr. William (Bill) Rippy. As of 2004, Holden's great-grandson, Dr. Wesley Rippy, continues the family legacy and mission of Christian health care in Oregon.

Along with Holden, Ralph Nelson, business manager/administrator from 1918 to 1955, helped lay a strong foundation for what the San would become. In 1944 he was the first Adventist hospital leader to be named administrator. During his tenure he saw the hospital through many changes and at least two major crises—paying off debt from the 1903 construction and rebuilding the sanitarium in the early 1920s.

Within a year of paying off the 1903 construction debt in 1919, Mount Tabor was annexed to Portland, and the city fire department condemned the top two floors of the wooden structure. The last patient was admitted on August 31, 1920, and the sanitarium closed. Wasting no time, Nelson rallied the community and church to raise $90,000 for a 50-bed replacement facility on the Mt. Tabor site.

The new hospital opened none too soon. Even before the painters and plasterers had completed their work, Holden performed an emergency appendectomy in the new operating room. Various expansion projects followed from 1924 through the early 1960s. With the exception of the 1964 expansion, all were funded primarily from operating surplus.

By the late 1960s, the Portland San again needed to expand. Not only was the Mt. Tabor site too small, but it was located on the side of an extinct volcano, and the soil was not suitable for supporting a large hospital. After learning of the availability of the 232-acre Glendoveer Golf Course, hospital leaders bought the property for $3 million intending to use part of the land for the hospital and to develop the remainder into a championship golf course and driving range. The community adamantly opposed the idea.

Mardian Blair became administrator in 1970 and set out to gain community support for the Glendoveer project. The management team united, even distributing informational brochures and soliciting signatures in support of the new hospital.

"It was a tough job," recalled Don Ammon, former executive vice president at Portland. "I remember day after day, evening after evening, going door to door around Glendoveer to see if I could get signatures from those living nearby."

The matter was controversial, requiring people to balance their loyalty to the hospital with their personal views about their neighborhood. Among those so affected was Dr. Eldon Snow, whose home backed up to the golf course. While he supported the hospital's position in whatever way he could, he had to be careful not to raise the ire of his neighbors.

In addition to the community relations issue, there was a long certificate-of-need and land-use process to undergo. Although the hospital had received a certificate of need for its new facility, after a two-and-a-half-year struggle, the county planning commission reversed an earlier decision and denied the land-use permit. Before it was all over, proponents and opponents shared their opinion in court.

"It was like a trial in city hall," recalled Ammon. "There were testimonies, cross examinations, and expert witnesses."

In the end, the county refunded the hospital the $3 million it had paid for the property. It continues to operate the golf course to this day.

God had a better plan for the hospital's location. About the time the county denied permission to build a hospital on the Glendoveer property, 40 acres in a prime location, with easy access to the proposed new Interstate 205, became available. The hospital bought the land and broke ground in 1974. A physicians' office building opened in 1976, and the new Adventist Medical Center opened in 1977. Additional professional buildings have been built in recent years. The Mt. Tabor hospital was eventually converted into a convalescent facility, and the oldest portion of the original 1922 sanitarium was demolished in 1980.

Today's 302-bed medical center is a testimony to the contribution made in the name of Christian health care in Portland, Oregon. Former CEO Larry Dodds commented, "We were able through the years to recruit people who had a genuine interest in creating a supportive environment where mission and spiritual care were paramount. The nurses and other staff have created a unique difference because of the continued emphasis on spiritual care for years and years."

SOURCES

Judd, Wayne, tape recorded interviews with Don Ammon, Frank Dupper, and Erwin Remboldt, 1998.

"Portland Adventist Through The Years," 1993.

Interviews: Larry Dodds and Monty Knittel.

The new hospital opened none too soon. Even before the painters and plasterers had completed their work, Holden performed an emergency appendectomy in the new operating room. Various expansion projects followed from 1924 through the early 1960s.

Retreat for the Sick and Tired

Walla Walla General Hospital: Walla Walla, Washington | Founded 1899

Dr. Isaac Dunlap and his wife Maggie, a nurse, returned to the Walla Walla Valley in 1899 after completing their studies in Battle Creek. The doctor had just graduated with the first class from American Medical Missionary College. Their mission in this rural Washington community in the "Valley of Many Waters" was the beginning of today's Walla Walla General Hospital.

Seventh-day Adventists had opened a college in Walla Walla in 1892, and the Dunlaps, upon their arrival in 1899, started treatment rooms in the basement of the administration building. In addition to providing hydrotherapy and other therapies, they also offered a medical missionary course, which 12 young people completed in 1900.

Three years later the Dunlaps built a house on College Avenue that served as both their residence and a sanitarium for the college. Along with conventional treatments of the day, they encouraged a balanced program of physical exercise, rest, sunshine, fresh air, a vegetarian diet, and trust in God. They planted a large garden where patients could relax and work outdoors.

For a while the doctor split his time between Walla Walla and the Mountain View Sanitarium in Spokane. Unfortunately, the Spokane structure burned in 1904. Rather than rebuild, the undamaged equipment was moved to Walla Walla and the two operations merged. This new Walla Walla Sanitarium rented space in a college dormitory, described as follows in a 1906 brochure:

The Walla Walla Sanitarium is located at College Place in the beautiful Walla Walla Valley, which is one of the finest fruit sections of the United States. In the springtime one can stand on the verandah and look out on the celebrated Blalock Fruit Ranch of thirteen hundred acres, four hundred of which are large bearing trees. When these are in bloom one looks upon a veritable sea of flowers. It is hard to find a more pleasant place in the spring than surrounds the sanitarium.

The sanitarium was again relocated in 1907. The College Place public schoolhouse was moved onto the college campus, hoisted on jacks, and given a new floor. This structure was expanded three times, and by the 1920s it had been transformed into a two-story facility with white pillars and wide verandahs. The advertising slogan of that era was, "A Retreat for the Sick and Tired."

With the purchase of a bankrupt hospital on Bonsella Street for $75,000, the San moved off the college campus in 1931. The facility was fully equipped with the latest in medical supplies, but it also came with an unpaid grocery bill for $20,000.

The sanitarium struggled through the 1930s by trimming salaries and personnel and cutting costs where possible. Telephone calls were limited to those deemed most essential. Business picked up in the 1940s, and by the end of 1950 plans were underway to expand. Other expansion projects followed, but by the 1970s hospital leaders decided to build an entirely new campus rather than continue adding to the Bonsella building.

Ron Sackett moved to Walla Walla from White Memorial Medical Center in Los Angeles in 1973. When he arrived, he found the average age of the medical staff to be about 67, only $60,000 in the bank, and the need for a new hospital. His first tasks, therefore, were to develop the medical staff and raise money for a new facility.

Disappointed to learn that the land was not for sale, they agreed to make it a matter of prayer. A few days later they went back to the owners, this time explaining their plans to build a hospital. The owners said they had been saving the property for just such a project.

He soon realized that the proposed location for the new hospital—on the grounds of the local Veteran's Administration—was unsatisfactory. The site had no surrounding population, no physicians' offices, and no convenient transportation. Accompanied by other Adventist health care officials, Sackett took an airplane ride over the area to take a look at the concentration of population and physicians' offices. They found a piece of land with better access to such essentials and sought out the owners to try to purchase it.

The Adventists did not discuss who they were or how they wanted to use the 18-acre property. They simply asked if the land was available for purchase. Disappointed to learn that the area was not for sale, the group agreed to make it a matter of prayer. A few days later they went back to the owners, this time divulging their plans to build a hospital. The owners miraculously revealed that they had been saving the property for just such a project.

As building began, the hospital found nearby Walla Walla College to be an invaluable resource for saving on construction costs. The engineering department faculty, headed by Professor Fred Bennett, helped plan and design the facility. As a result, the hospital was built at a cost of $4.5 million—only $55 per square foot. The grand opening on July 10, 1977, drew a crowd of about 3,000.

Along with conventional treatments of the day, they encouraged a balanced program of physical exercise, rest, sunshine, fresh air, a vegetarian diet, and trust in God. They planted a large garden where patients could relax and work outdoors.

Today Walla Walla General Hospital is a 72-bed facility with a level III trauma-certified emergency center serving an area of nearly 60,000 residents. While many changes have occurred over the years, the hospital continues the mission begun more than a century ago by a young couple from Battle Creek.

SOURCES

Benton, Pat Horning, "Staying Well Is Better than Getting Well," *North Pacific Union Gleaner*, May 21, 1999.

Benton, Pat Horning, "Celebrating a Century of Caring and Sharing," *A Century of Care*, Walla Walla General Hospital, June 6, 1999.

Chappel, Heather, "History Script," 1999.

Interview: Ron Sackett.

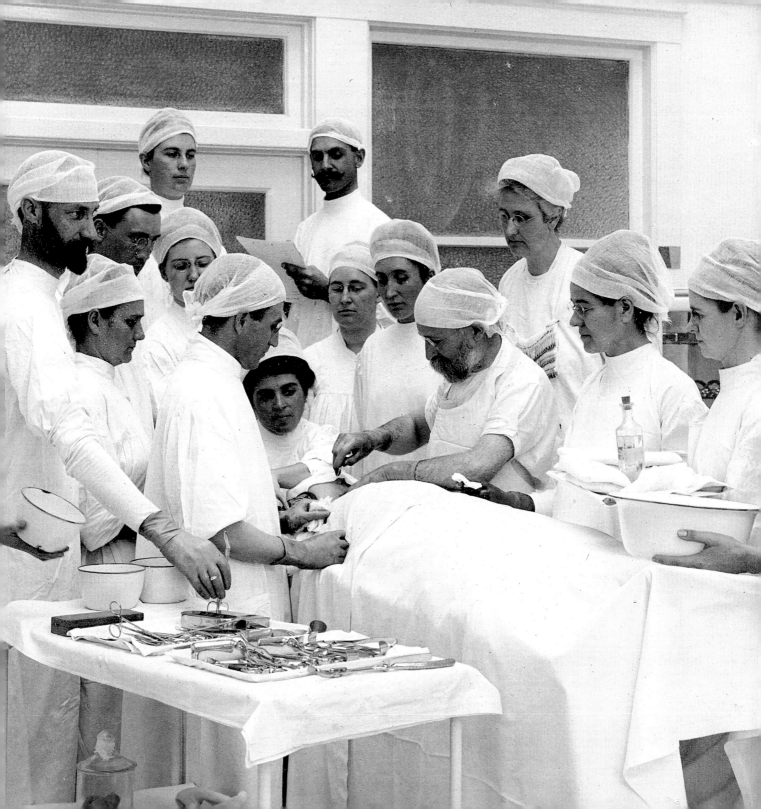

Wheel of Providence Turns

Paradise Valley Hospital: National City, California | 1904–2007

In 1901 Ellen G. White told Dr. T.S. Whitelock about her interest in opening a sanitarium in the San Diego area. A nationwide financial depression in the 1890s had made available—at very attractive prices—a number of resort properties in Southern California. Mrs. White believed these offered excellent opportunities for the church to expand its healing mission.

Whitelock, a graduate of the American Medical Missionary College in Battle Creek, along with Sophie Johnson operated a successful treatment center in San Diego. A short time after Dr. Whitelock's conversation with Mrs. White, one of his patients told him about an abandoned sanitarium in nearby National City. Dr. Anna Mary Longshore Potts, a woman of Quaker heritage, had developed the 20-acre property, which consisted of a main building, residence, stable, and cottage for employees. Soon after the facility opened in 1888, the region experienced a prolonged and severe drought. Wells all over the area dried up, once-profitable businesses closed, and people moved away. Potts closed the sanitarium and turned it over to her uncle, Dr. T.H. Harrison of New York. He put it on the market for $28,000.

By the time Mrs. White visited the site, it had been abandoned for about 14 years. Most of the trees and shrubs had died, and bats occupied the main building. Nevertheless, she said she had never seen a building better adapted to be a sanitarium. The main structure had about 50 rooms and a large verandah where patients could relax and enjoy the view.

However, not everyone shared Whitelock and Mrs. White's eagerness to start a health facility in National City. The church's small Southern California Conference numbered fewer than 1,200 members and was already $40,000 in debt. In addition, the denomination's world headquarters, the General Conference of Seventh-day Adventists, was already financially strapped due to its early medical work, and no one had any intention of incurring more debt for health care facilities.

Whitelock managed to negotiate Harrison's price down to $8,000, but the deal still remained out of reach for the Southern California Conference.

"The Lord would not give us an elephant without providing water for it to drink." And when his workers finally did reach water, it proved to be a gully-washer. Water poured in so quickly that they did not even stop to gather their tools before scrambling out of the well.

Meanwhile, Mrs. White and her friend Josephine Gotzian, a generous contributor to other church organizations, each agreed to come up with $2,000, not knowing where they might get the remaining $4,000. But they were undaunted. Mrs. White recalled,

> *A special opportunity came to us in the form of a property a few miles south of San Diego known as the Potts Sanitarium. The Lord had manifestly prepared the way for us to begin sanitarium work at this point; and when the wheel of providence turned in our favor, and the property came within our reach, we felt as if we must act without further delay, notwithstanding the hesitancy of brethren in responsibility, who should have been quick to discern the advantages of this place as a center for medical missionary work.*

Still keenly interested in the sanitarium despite the financial obstacles, Whitelock, as well as other potential buyers, frequently visited the Potts property. On one occasion in January 1904, the doctor struck up a conversation with a woman at the site. When he introduced himself, she seemed surprised.

"You are the very person I'm looking for," she said.

Harrison had sent her, in fact, to ask Whitelock for an offer. She suggested $6,000, but the doctor had only $4,000. His offer was wired to Harrison, who immediately accepted it. Within a matter of hours, another party offered $6,000 for the property, but Harrison stuck to his agreement with Whitelock.

With help from a family who paid the back taxes and purchased eight additional acres, Paradise Valley Sanitarium began with an investment of less than $6,000. A stock company was formed to raise funds with the idea that the Southern California Conference would eventually take it over.

The first order of business was to repair the run-down facility and, most importantly, find a water source. E.R. Palmer, acquainted with Mrs. White from her work in Australia, managed the new venture in National City. Although repairs were extensive, Palmer spent as little money as possible. He reportedly mended a shingle roof with small pieces of tin cans and took advantage of good deals on high-quality furniture made of bird's-eye maple.

The founders of Paradise Valley Sanitarium knew the most important find, however, would be water. Hopes must have dimmed as the drought continued through the summer of 1904. At Mrs. White's recommendation, Palmer hired a well digger from Nebraska. Digging the well turned into a long, slow process, but the team's faith held strong. Mrs. White asked the well driller, Salem Hamilton, what he planned to do after digging more than 80 feet and finding nothing.

"Did the Lord tell you to buy the property?" he asked.

"Yes, and not just once but three times," she insisted.

Harrison's reply became forever etched in the history of Paradise Valley Hospital: "The Lord would not give us an elephant without providing water for it to drink."

When his workers finally reached water, it proved to be a gully-washer, sending them scrambling for dry land without even stopping to gather their tools.

Guests began arriving before repairs were completed, and on opening day the sanitarium already had 20 patients. Although Paradise Valley attracted a large clientele, the first couple of years were difficult.

To further complicate matters, the opening of two other Southern California facilities in Glendale and Loma Linda greatly hindered recruitment at Paradise Valley because employees preferred to work at the new church-owned sanitariums. To meet this challenge, Mrs. White personally solicited funds for the sanitarium and published a brochure detailing God's providential leading in the purchase of the property. Paradise Valley was also among the facilities to benefit from the sale of her book, *Ministry of Healing.*

Frequent management changes and medical staff turnover hurt the sanitarium's reputation in the early years. However, through persistence and hard work, Paradise Valley finally showed a profit in 1910, and ownership transferred to the Southern California Conference in 1912. John Burden, who had served at St. Helena and Sydney and had been instrumental in obtaining the properties at Glendale and Loma Linda, managed Paradise Valley Sanitarium from 1916 to 1924 and again from 1925 to 1934.

A.C. Larson led Paradise Valley Sanitarium through many challenges during his administration from 1934 to 1944. The years of the Great Depression and World War II called for unusual methods to meet the financial requirements of running a hospital. Once when he needed $3,000 for payroll, Larson called his key leaders and asked them to join him in his office. They were kneeling in prayer when Larson's secretary entered the room and tapped him on the shoulder. She handed him a note saying that a woman had just given the hospital a check for $3,000.

Though growth continued through the 1950s, the 1960s marked big changes for Paradise Valley with the opening of a new 150-bed replacement hospital in 1966. Also, the last nursing class graduated in 1967. Programs and facilities continued to be added as the hospital grew to meet the needs of the diverse communities in the San Diego area.

As many industry and market forces impacted the hospital's ability to thrive, Adventist Health's board of directors made the difficult decision in 2007 to transfer ownership of the organization.

SOURCES

Johns, Warren L., and Richard H. Utt, editors. *The Vision Bold,* Washington, D.C.: Review and Herald Publishing Association, 1977.

Judd, Wayne R., and Jonathan M. Butler, editors. *Thirsty Elephant: The Story of Paradise Valley Hospital,* National City, California: Paradise Valley Hospital, 1994.

White, Ellen G., *The Paradise Valley Sanitarium*, Mountain View, Calif.: Pacific Press Publishing Association, 1909.

Interview: Mardian Blair.

Burden's Twenty-Dollar Deal

Glendale Adventist Medical Center: Glendale, California | Founded 1905

After successfully moving ahead without church backing at Paradise Valley, Ellen G. White began pressing for the purchase of another property. Still convinced that the church risked missing some real bargains following the depression of the 1890s, she urged leaders to build another sanitarium in Southern California. Growing impatient over their reluctance to act, she asked her friend John Burden to look at available properties in Los Angeles. She was well acquainted with his work at

St. Helena Sanitarium in California and Sydney Sanitarium in Australia. As for Burden, he trusted White implicitly. When faced with a difficult decision of whether to heed her counsel or follow instruction from church leaders, Burden could be counted on to side with her.

He found a number of likely locations in the Los Angeles area, the most promising being the 75-room Glendale Hotel. Located on a five-acre plot and built at a cost of $60,000, the facility had never opened as a hotel. It had housed a school for a short time, but it stood empty when Burden found it on the market for $26,000 in 1904.

The quiet country town of Glendale with about 500 residents was ideal for a sanitarium. There was even an electric car line running past the property, providing easy access to Los Angeles. But despite the site's perfect attributes and bargain price, Burden knew church leaders would not agree to buy it. After much personal deliberation, he determined that if the realtor dropped the price to $15,000, he would consider it a sign from the Lord and move ahead with the purchase.

Realtor Leslie Brand represented the property's seller and was probably the most notable figure in the early development of the Glendale area. Burden told him of the plan to build a facility similar to the famous Battle Creek Sanitarium, and when he said the church didn't have much money, Brand dropped the price to $12,500— $2,500 less than Burden was prepared to pay. According to legend, Burden immediately handed Brand a $20 bill to seal the deal, having no idea where he would get the rest of the money. This providential relationship with

It was majestic with its parlor, dining room, solarium, and manicured landscape. The zoo was fascinating with monkeys, bears, deer, and other animals. The huge powerhouse was impressive. To the families from Michigan it was a poor substitute for the Battle Creek Sanitarium, but we could not imagine anything grander than the new Glendale Sanitarium and Hospital.

Brand continued to bear fruit, as he was instrumental in the removal of a stipulation prohibiting the use of the property for a sanitarium.

While a $20 bill may have secured the property for purchase, Burden still needed the money for the down payment. At that time, the Southern California Conference of Seventh-day Adventists numbered just over 1,000 members and held around $40,000 in debt. Not surprisingly, therefore, and as Burden predicted, the church constituency voted against the purchase. Fortunately, Conference President Clarence Santee shared Burden's conviction that the opportunity to buy the hotel at that price likely would never come again. He decided to take a leap of faith and join Burden in personally advancing the down payment, although neither of them had any idea of how the balance would be paid.

From her home in Northern California, Mrs. White wrote to conference leaders who were meeting in Washington, D.C., urging them to buy the Glendale property. When Santee read her letter aloud, they immediately pledged $5,200. With $1,000 advances from two other church members, the conference made a $4,500 cash payment, put the rest in a bank, and paid the balance over the next three years.

Burden became manager and immediately set to work with a group of volunteers, who had Glendale's first medical facility mopped, scrubbed, sterilized, painted, and ready for business in August 1905. Soon guests were enjoying what an early brochure described as "the fruit-laden valleys of the 'Land of Sunshine and Flowers.'"

To meet staffing needs, the sanitarium began training nurses with a strict regimen based on the principle of hard work and low pay. Student nurses received six cents an hour during their first year, and 10 cents in their second year. Nothing was to interfere with sleep, studies, or work—certainly not parties, recreation, or courtships. By the time the nursing program transferred to Pacific Union College in 1967, the Glendale Adventist Hospital had graduated 1,282 nurses.

As Glendale's population boomed to nearly 30,000 by the early 1920s, the sanitarium outgrew its original facility. The property was sold for $250,000 dollars, of which $50,000 was used to buy 30 acres for a replacement hospital. Construction began immediately on a hill of apricot groves between the San Rafael foothills and the Sierra Madres. Unfortunately, costs soared to more than a million dollars. A major reorganization put Burden in charge again, and the new sanitarium opened in March 1924. The debt, however, would not be paid off until the late 1930s.

Local resident Dr. Robert Horner remembered the facility as follows:

> *I grew up in the Glendale San community during the 1930s, a few years after the hospital relocated to Chevy Chase Drive. It was majestic with its parlor, dining room, solarium, and manicured landscape. The zoo was fascinating with monkeys, bears, deer, and other animals. The huge powerhouse was impressive. To the families from Michigan it was a poor substitute for the Battle Creek Sanitarium, but we could not imagine anything grander than the new Glendale Sanitarium and Hospital.*

Expansion continued and new services were added over the next several decades, keeping pace with the growing city. Two key figures during this time were George Nelson, administrator from 1947 to 1959, and Erwin Remboldt, administrator from 1960 to 1973. During Nelson's administration the hospital celebrated its 50th anniversary with the opening of a new wing, bringing the total patient beds to 292.

By the early 1960s most of the Glendale San's business was acute-care, with only a few long-term sanitarium patients. The hospital was the largest in the city and enjoyed an excellent reputation. While it was rapidly moving away from the sanitarium business, the facility continued to maintain some features from the by-gone days, such as an aviary and a small zoo with several monkeys.

The zoo finally gave way to new construction when a 60-bed mental health unit opened in 1963. The expansion was paid for in part with Hill-Burton funding, one of the first times government assistance was used to underwrite Adventist health initiatives.

Other significant developments came about during Remboldt's administration. A civic advisory board recommended removing the word "Sanitarium" from the facility name because it no longer reflected the hospital's business. When it was changed to Glendale Adventist Hospital on January 1, 1966, the hospital became the first in the United States to use "Adventist" in its name. Also in 1966 Glendale Adventist was the first private hospital in Los Angeles to install the new 1440 IBM computer. A year later, construction on the Ventura Freeway ate up 3.5 acres of hospital property, and ground was broken for a $3.5 million diagnostic and treatment center.

In 1972 church leaders asked Remboldt to organize a corporation of Adventist hospitals in California, Arizona, Hawaii, and Utah. He left the hospital in October 1973 to devote attention to this organization, originally known as Adventist Health Services. Discussions around uniting Adventist hospitals had been going on for some time. The large for-profit hospital corporations were posing a real threat to the church's many stand-alone hospitals. Binding together would give them increased purchasing power, management expertise, economies of scale, and marketing clout they lacked on their own. Remboldt pioneered the system of Adventist hospitals in the western United States, and one of his first tasks was to set up an office for Adventist Health Services.

"We found a place down on Chevy Chase," he later recalled. "I think it had four or five rooms. The secretary and I sat there the first day. We got two phone calls."

The calm did not last long, because he soon began meeting with various hospital board members, trying to convince them to turn over their hospitals to this new organization—a job he described as "no small feat." The first programs Adventist Health Services organized were malpractice insurance, purchasing, and internal auditing.

Time brought more changes to the Glendale hospital. A family practice residency program began in 1973. The main building of the 1923 hospital was replaced in the mid-1970s, and the name was changed to Glendale Adventist Medical Center in 1975. Today Glendale Adventist Medical

Center is a 515-bed state-of-the-art medical facility with the same focus on improving the health of its community by sharing God's love through healing and wellness as when it began in 1905.

SOURCES

Johns, Warren L., and Richard H. Utt, editors, *The Vision Bold*, Washington, D.C.: Review and Herald Publishing Association, 1977.

Judd, Wayne, tape recorded interviews with Don Ammon, Frank Dupper and Erwin Remboldt, 1998.

Interviews and Notes: Dr. Robert Horner and George Nelson.

Not for Any Common Purpose

Loma Linda University Health: Loma Linda, California | Founded 1905

When it became obvious that the differences between church leaders and Dr. John Harvey Kellogg at Battle Creek could not be reconciled, Ellen G. White began looking for another location for a medical school. She urged church leaders to explore some bargain properties in Southern California. Finally, a committee headed by John Burden, business manager of the Glendale Sanitarium, found a likely location near San Bernardino—a 76-acre resort called Loma Linda with a hotel, farmhouse, cottages, amusement center, and other buildings. A group of businessmen and physicians had paid $15,000 for the property, and after investing another $155,000 in it, suffered a downturn in business during the 1890s. Some even nicknamed it "Lonesome Linda."

When Burden found the property on the market for $110,000, he knew it was far more than the church could afford—even if leaders ignored their pay-as-you-go policy. With the recent establishment of the Glendale Sanitarium, the church's Southern California Conference had no money, and many church members who might have had the means to invest had already put their money into the Paradise Valley project near San Diego.

Even when the price dropped to $85,000, Burden could not consider it. But, when it came down to $40,000, he wrote to Mrs. White, who was in Washington, D.C., at the time. She told him, "Secure the property by all means. This is the very property we ought to have."

Members of the local church conference were not so enthusiastic, however. With some committee members away in Washington at the time, those back in California did not feel at liberty to spend that kind of money without consulting their colleagues. They wired Washington and received a prompt-but-negative response.

What should Burden do? Mrs. White said go, and the brethren said no. More wires were exchanged between Washington and California until the order came, signed by Mrs. White, to do nothing until the church leaders returned to California. She later told Burden she could not ask the church to take on additional debt.

Burden knew that in her heart Mrs. White did not want to wait. She had once assured him that the money would come from unexpected sources, and he believed with all his heart that it would. He tried to get an extension on the option to buy the property, but the owners insisted on $1,000 in earnest money. Yet another message came from Washington: "Developments do not warrant securing Loma Linda." Fearing he would lose the sale, however, Burden signed the papers in his own name and bought the property.

When Mrs. White saw Loma Linda for the first time, she was delighted with it:

> *The Lord has not given us this property for any common purpose…*
>
> *With the possession of this place comes the weighty responsibility of making the work of the institution educational in character. A school is to be established here for the training of gospel medical missionary evangelists. Much is involved in this work, and it is very essential that a right beginning be made. The Lord has a special work to be done in this part of the field.*

Meanwhile, Burden had payments due, and his appeals to area churches seemed to generate more controversy than money. After the denomination's vice president, G.A. Irwin, began asking church members for assistance, gifts began coming—many from unexpected sources. One woman pledged $10,000. A letter from Atlantic City, New Jersey, contained $5,000. Another from Oregon contained $4,500. Within seven months the entire note was paid. With a discount for early payment, plus interest and taxes, Loma Linda was purchased for less than $46,000.

The new owners immediately began making repairs and renovations. Even though the Loma Linda Sanitarium did not officially open until November 1905, patients began arriving in October. It was dedicated in April 1906, subsequently named Loma Linda College of Evangelists, and within only eight months, posted a gain of $1,160.

It took time to clarify the nature of the new college because some thought it was to train medical missionaries in simple treatments such as hydrotherapy and massage, while others believed it must be an accredited school for training fully qualified physicians. Ellen G. White's comment that the school was to be "of the highest order" gave leaders a clear directive.

The name was changed to the College of Medical Evangelists (CME) and the newly appointed leaders included Dr. Wells Allen Ruble, President; Dr. George K. Abbott, Dean; John Burden,

Business Manager; and G.A. Irwin, Board Chairman. The first faculty members were mostly former teachers and graduates of American Medical Missionary College in Battle Creek.

Until the early 1900s, almost anyone could start a medical school in the United States, and these institutions were cranking out diplomas almost as fast as they could print them. Some schools did not even require a high school diploma for admission. The best schools offered only 24 months of training.

In an effort to close some of these schools and upgrade the professional training for physicians, the American Medical Association established a rating system. Most states allowed only graduates of A and B schools to take their board examinations, leaving a degree from a C-rated school virtually worthless.

Although representatives of the rating organization recommended that the College of Medical Evangelists be closed in 1912, school leaders would not think of it. They continued with limited resources but great faith. One of the biggest problems was finding sufficient clinical experience for the students at Loma Linda. As a solution, the school set up a program with the Los Angeles County Hospital and also opened a dispensary in Los Angeles. Yet in spite of these efforts, CME received a C rating in 1914.

Some considered this proof enough that the church should exit the medical school business. Others suggested cutting back to a two-year curriculum. Finally the clinical program in Los

"The Lord has not given us this property for any common purpose... A school is to be established here for the training of gospel medical missionary evangelists. Much is involved in this work, and it is very essential that a right beginning be made."

– ELLEN G. WHITE

Angeles was strengthened and the four-year program continued. When the decision was made in 1915 to build White Memorial Medical Center as a clinical site for the medical school, President Evans recommended that Dr. Percy Magan, his former associate at Madison College in Tennessee, be invited to develop the Los Angeles campus. Magan accepted the position of dean and led the school through challenges that he said were "beset with difficulties from every side."

Magan was the kind of person who made a big difference in whatever he did. Born in Ireland in 1867, he moved to the United States in his teens and became a Seventh-day Adventist. He soon attracted the attention of Nellie Druillard, a teacher and church official in Nebraska, who encouraged him to attend Battle Creek College. There he met Druillard's nephew, Edward Sutherland, who became his lifelong friend, colleague, and confidant.

Magan knew that the future of Adventist hospitals depended on having qualified physicians. Developing CME into an A-level school was a huge challenge as he dealt with faculty and organizational issues, accreditation, fundraising, and attitudes ranging from indifference to outright opposition.

When Magan told his friend Sutherland he needed $60,000 to build White Memorial Medical Center, Sutherland arranged to send $50,000 from Madison. The medical school board authorized the purchase of half a block of property in the Boyle Heights area of Los Angeles. Knowing it was far too small, Magan told Evans one day that he would not show his Irish face again until he had the money to buy the rest of the block. (When the board later reprimanded him for buying the additional land without authorization, he insisted that their disapproval was a small price to pay for the future of the school.)

Although the property was still undeveloped, Magan took Dr. Nathan P. Colwell to see it. Colwell had been a member of the committee that advised Adventists to give up the school in 1912. As the two men looked at the "mass of weeds, cockleburs, and…two or three sorry-looking animals" feeding on the property, Magan told him that one day a great medical organization would occupy the site.

During World War I the C-rated school was at risk of losing some faculty and students to the draft, which could jeopardize its future. Magan knew if the school closed it would never reopen. He personally visited the Surgeon General in Washington, D.C. and the medical school rating agency in Chicago. It took some creative negotiating and answers to prayer, but in the end CME received an early inspection and the B classification it needed for students and faculty to be deferred from the draft.

The school faced another crisis in 1921 when an accrediting committee found it to be weak in several key areas, citing the school for having a divided campus, an insufficient budget, and a lack of research facilities. It took much persuasion and many prayers, but the necessary changes were made, and the medical school finally received an A classification in 1922. No one was more surprised than Colwell.

The 1960s saw major changes for the school, which was renamed Loma Linda University in 1961. Under Dr. David Hinshaw's direction, the two-campus arrangement ended by relocating the clinical programs to Loma Linda.

The opening of the $20 million Loma Linda University Medical Center in 1967 marked a new era for the organization. In the book *Legacy*, author Richard A. Schaefer reported that within the next 30 years the hospital grew by 600 percent.

The Loma Linda University Heart Surgery Team performed a special heart surgery that gained Loma Linda University Medical Center international attention in 1984. The name Baby Fae became permanently etched in the history books of medical science when she received a transplantation of a baboon's heart. While the procedure drew both approval and condemnation, it was a landmark case.

"It has become a reference point in the public's awareness of hypoplastic left-heart syndrome and the serious efforts being made to save doomed babies," Schaffer wrote. "It became the cornerstone of a successful, international, infant-to-infant heart-transplant program begun in Loma Linda about a year later."

✳

The story begins shortly after the first successful human-heart transplant in 1967 by Dr. Christiaan Barnard in South Africa. Leonard Bailey, a medical student at Loma Linda, began studying heart transplantation in 1969. After medical school, he took a residency at the Hospital for Sick Children in Toronto, Canada, where he specialized in pediatric cardiac surgery. He was especially interested in hypoplastic left-heart syndrome, the underdevelopment of the left side of the heart. The fatal condition occurs about once in every 12,000 live births in the United States.

At Loma Linda, Dr. Bailey and his associates were seeing from six to eight babies die every year as a result of hypoplastic left-heart syndrome and began to look at transplantation as a solution. After six years of research and many months of working through the approval process, the door was finally opened for a cross-species transplant at Loma Linda.

A baby girl with hypoplastic left-heart syndrome was born prematurely in Barstow, California, in October 1984. The mother discussed the procedure at length with Bailey, and while he could give her no guarantee of success, she knew her baby had no other chance at life.

Many sophisticated and time-consuming tests were performed to find the best tissue-matched donor, during which time Baby Fae almost died. Meanwhile, the hospital's institutional review board monitored the situation closely, granting its final approval only two days before the surgery.

The baby's condition had stabilized by the time the test results were received at 4 a.m., Friday, October 26. The history-making surgery began at 6:30 a.m., taking doctors about one hour to implant the walnut-size heart in the baby's chest. By 11:35 a.m., it was beating on its own. Although Baby Fae lived only 20 days, she and her family made an immeasurable contribution in the effort to save babies born with a fatal abnormality.

Except for the hill on which it was built, today's Loma Linda University bears no resemblance to the "Lonesome Linda" health resort of the early 1900s, and the changes continue. In May of 2016, Loma Linda began construction of a new acute care adult tower and children's hospital tower to open in 2020. Standing 16 floors and spanning a distance longer than a football field, the new facility will contain a first-of-its-kind vertical earthquake isolation system designed to keep the hospital operational following a potentially catastrophic magnitude 7.9 earthquake on the nearby San Jacinto Fault.

Tens of thousands have graduated from the university's schools of medicine, dentistry, public health, nursing, and allied health. Clearly, Loma Linda University and Loma Linda University Health bear witness to the statement made nearly a century ago that God did not provide this place for any common purpose.

SOURCES

Gish, Ira, and Harry Christman, *Madison—God's Beautiful Farm*, Nampa, Idaho: The Upward Way, 1989.

Johns, Warren L., and Richard H. Utt, editors, *The Vision Bold*, Washington, D.C.: Review and Herald Publishing Association, 1977.

Neff, Merlin L., *For God and C.M.E.*, Mountain View, California: Pacific Press Publishing Association, 1964.

Schaefer, Richard A., *Legacy: Daring to Care,* Loma Linda, California: Legacy Publishing Association, 1995.

Utt, Richard, *From Vision to Reality*, Loma Linda, California: Loma Linda University, 1980.

Interviews and Notes: William Murrill.

When David Paulson Prayed

Adventist Medical Center Hinsdale: Hinsdale, Illinois | Founded 1905

HINSDALE SANITARIUM AND HOSPITAL
HINSDALE ILLINOIS

Adventist health care in Chicago was a by-product of Dr. John Harvey Kellogg's work in Battle Creek. It started in 1892 when a wealthy man hired a nurse to work among Chicago's poor. Sometime later, John Wessels, a Seventh-day Adventist whose family had made a fortune in the diamond mines of South Africa, asked Kellogg what he would do if he were to receive a large amount of money. When Kellogg said he would open a mission for the poor in Chicago, Wessels handed him a check for $40,000.

Meanwhile, the young man who would eventually direct this mission work and establish Adventist Medical Center Hinsdale was studying at the University of Michigan. David Paulson had attended Battle Creek College and, in 1891, was one of several students selected to study medicine at the University of Michigan. Paulson's interest in the field of medicine occurred several years earlier, however, when he fell ill during a diphtheria outbreak in his childhood home of South Dakota. In the book, *His Name was David*, Paulson's sister-in-law, Caroline Louise Clough, described how the illness devastated the Paulson family:

> *"Martin is dead. You must help me carry him out," David heard his father tell one of his brothers.*
>
> *When they returned to the house, the sick boy heard his father's voice again.*
>
> *"David will be next. He can't last long. I think we had better wait and bury both boys at once."*
>
> *As he lay in bed, David promised that if he were allowed to live, he would devote his life to helping the sick and suffering—a promise he faithfully kept throughout his lifetime.*

From Ann Arbor, Paulson moved to New York City to complete his studies at Bellevue Medical College. He worked in the medical mission operated by Dr. George Dowknott in the slums of New York, and during this time he visited many homes where people had little food and knew few of the comforts of life. It made a lasting impression on him.

When he left New York, Paulson joined the Chicago mission work, which grew rapidly with clinics, dispensaries, a branch sanitarium, a home for unwed mothers and their babies, a men's mission, a magazine, and much more. It soon was large enough to provide clinical practice for medical students at the new American Medical Missionary College, which opened in 1895 with campuses in both Battle Creek and Chicago.

Paulson's fervent prayers throughout his life for both large and small needs proved to be the lifeline for the Chicago mission's work. For example, one day he prayed for a stenographer to record his lectures to Medical Missionary College students. Only a couple of days later, a man in ragged clothes came asking for work. At first the doctor was sure he had no job for the unkempt man.

"'I'm a stenographer, sir,'" the man said.

Without hesitating, the two men knelt and thanked God for bringing them together. This man turned out to be an outstanding stenographer, who could recall Paulson's lectures almost verbatim without taking notes.

One day Paulson and a patient named C.B. Kimbell were talking about the mission's work for unwed mothers. The facility for these women was located in an area with many saloons and brothels, and most of the mothers returned to the very lifestyles that had brought them to the mission in the first place. Paulson needed a place outside the city for the women and their babies. Kimbell offered him a house in Hinsdale, which proved to be an excellent solution and the first of many positive influences Kimbell made on Adventist health care in Chicago.

The Chicago mission work lost its financial support after the Battle Creek Sanitarium burned in 1902, and it was clear that Adventist health care in that city must take another direction. Expressing concern that the mission work was a financial drain on the denomination, Ellen G. White called for a balanced approach to health services that would provide for the needy, yet at the same time attract a clientele that could pay for services.

Paulson was firmly committed to the poor, and he feared that this aspect of the church's mission would be lost if it built a sanitarium that catered to the wealthy. At one point he made an impassioned plea to board members, saying he was "determined there shall be one spot left on this selfish earth where a man can have a helping hand extended to him whether he has money or not." Once again, his friend Kimbell came up with a solution—build a sanitarium first for those who can pay, then establish a facility for the sick poor.

Sometime later Kimbell took Paulson and his wife to see a property that he believed might be suitable for a sanitarium. It was the Judge Beckwith home, a 10-acre wooded estate in Hinsdale with a 15-room house, plus another nine-room structure and plenty of outbuildings. The $16,000 price tag certainly was right, but the Paulsons had not one penny available to buy it. A few days later Kimbell came back with an offer.

"I'll buy the property and deed it to you on the condition that you pay for it in 20 annual installments, without interest," he said.

Plans for the sanitarium continued, as did the answered prayers. Shortly before Hinsdale Sanitarium opened, Dr. Paulson needed to pay some bills, and so he borrowed $5,000 from a wealthy Hinsdale resident named Dr. Pearsons. Paulson later needed another $5,000, and Pearsons loaned the funds once again—on the condition that the entire $10,000 be repaid by April 1.

Two weeks before the deadline, Pearsons asked the doctor whether he had the money. Paulson said no, but assured him he would have it by April 1.

"Where can you get it?" Pearsons asked, to which Paulson replied that he would look for the Lord to provide it.

Two days before the April 1 deadline, a sanitarium visitor approached the doctor after morning worship. She said she expected to receive $5,000 and thought perhaps he could use it. A few hours later Pearsons showed up at the business office, announcing that he had persuaded a local bank to loan the sanitarium $5,000. With the money the woman had promised, Paulson had all he needed to repay Pearsons in full.

Not long afterwards, Paulson lacked $1,000 to complete the facility's roof. Once again he called the sanitarium family together to pray. A few days later he received a letter with a check.

"I hear you are trying to start a sanitarium in Hinsdale," the writer said. "I have just sold my farm and have $1,150 to place somewhere. I don't know why, but I felt compelled to send it to you."

The sanitarium opened in 1905, with the first patient arriving before the stairs were completed. Thanks to a dumb waiter that remained from the original construction, the staff lifted the patient to the upper floor.

By 1910 the College of Medical Evangelists had started in California and the American Medical Missionary College—with all the clinics and dispensaries connected with the Chicago Medical Mission—had closed. In that same year Paulson realized his dream of opening a facility on the sanitarium campus for the sick poor. He recalled:

> *As we were making our last enlargement of the sanitarium and building the Rescue Home, we felt the time had come to definitely establish our work for the sick poor, the Good Samaritan Inn…but strangely enough I could not get hold of any money to put in a heating plant…the house was cold and the patients had to be moved over to the sanitarium…It actually took us a couple of years more before we were again able to open our Good Samaritan Inn…When we did, a good woman gave us four hundred dollars without any solicitation, to make the necessary repairs….*
>
> *One night a stranger who happened to be here sent for me after I had gone home and wanted me to tell him about the Good Samaritan Inn, which I did. He wrote me a check for one hundred dollars. Next one of our patients, without my having mentioned the matter to her, sent me one hundred dollars for the same purpose, and another good woman gave me a hundred dollars.*

Paulson became gravely ill in 1916. After short stays at Madison, Tennessee, and Boulder, Colorado, the 48-year-old doctor moved near Asheville, North Carolina. However, his health was spent, and his condition gradually worsened. Two noteworthy visitors came to his bedside before he died, Dr. Percy Magan from Tennessee and cereal giant W.K. Kellogg, who paid for his funeral expenses and transportation back to Hinsdale.

One of the most noted chapters in Hinsdale history occurred during the polio epidemic in 1949. In one month alone, 13 cases were reported in the community, and the number approached 70 before the epidemic ended. People hated to hear their phones ring for fear it would be news of another polio case.

Eugene Kettering, son of inventor Charles F. Kettering, and his family had recently moved near the sanitarium when the son of one of their landscape workers was diagnosed with polio. At the time, the sanitarium was not equipped for this type of care, so he was taken to another hospital. A short time later, the Ketterings equipped a unit for contagious diseases at the sanitarium.

"Everyone wanted to do something," Virginia Kettering said. According to Ray Pelton, who worked at the hospital at that time, Mrs. Kettering asked her daughter what she wanted for Christmas that year.

"Mother, you know I don't need anything," the young girl replied.

"Yes, you do," Mrs. Kettering said. "You need three new iron lungs for the Hinsdale San to treat the polio patients."

Eugene Kettering personally arranged for the iron lungs to be transported and delivered to the Hinsdale San. The Ketterings went to the hospital every night, taking food the community had prepared for the staff. Describing the therapists as "the most beautiful people," Mrs. Kettering said she believed their care and attention made all the difference in the patients' progress.

By the end of the year, the Ketterings had organized a major fundraising effort to replace the old wooden structure in which the Paulsons had started the Hinsdale Sanitarium 50 years earlier. The new hospital opened in 1953.

Adventist Medical Center Hinsdale has been the starting place for a number of Adventist health care leaders, among them Ray Pelton. Immediately after graduating from Union College in Lincoln, Nebraska, young Pelton arrived at Hinsdale in 1949 expecting an entry-level position with some management responsibility. Instead, he became an orderly. It seems that the person in the position for which Pelton had been hired was in no hurry to move on. After two or three months serving as an orderly, Pelton was promoted to night admitting clerk—a job that taught him some valuable lessons in working with the public.

Paulson was firmly committed to the poor, and he feared that this aspect of the church's mission would be lost if it built a sanitarium that catered to the wealthy. At one point he made an impassioned plea to board members, saying he was "determined there shall be one spot left on this selfish earth where a man can have a helping hand extended to him whether he has money or not."

A.C. Larson was administrator of Hinsdale Sanitarium and Hospital from 1954 to 1963. Although he was regarded as a kind gentleman, he did not tolerate any foolishness. Pelton admits to having been corrected on occasion by the no-nonsense leader.

"He was democratic, but he called the shots," noted Pelton, recalling one employee's experience when Larson determined he needed to find another career opportunity. This man boasted that he had no intention of leaving his position.

"Administrators come and go, but I stay," the staff member said.

A few weeks later the employee did not receive a paycheck. Needless to say, he left Hinsdale and Larson stayed.

Larson was the first of nine Hinsdale administrators with whom Kathryn Sieberman, retired vice president, worked between 1957 and 1999. Each had his unique style and contributed to the hospital's success.

"Even though it seemed he was strictly all business, Mr. Larson had a very kind heart. He did things to help employees feel like family—picnics, corn roasts, watermelon feeds, Christmas parties, and Saturday night lyceums," said Sieberman.

Among her favorite memories of the Larson era were the visits of his brother-in-law, Harley Rice.

"He was 'Mr. Hospital' in the Adventist church in those days and traveled around the world helping medical institutions," she recalled. "He was also a poet and wrote about his travels. When he visited Hinsdale, Mr. Larson would invite him to have morning worship for the administrative staff, which occurred every morning promptly at eight o'clock in his office. Harley Rice would give us wonderful travelogues describing his visits to such places as Calcutta and Bangalore."

During the 1960s, Sieberman worked with Mardian Blair and Bill Wilson, two administrators who devoted a lot of effort to recruiting a strong team of employees.

"One of us might go to Madison, Wisconsin, another to Indianapolis, and another to Detroit. We'd stay for three to five days, calling every church elder within any reasonable distance to get names of members who might be potential employees—nurses, nurse's aides, cooks, accountants, secretaries. We'd come home from those trips with about 30 names," she explained. "Then we'd have to sort them out."

Anyone who has been around Adventist Medical Center Hinsdale for any time has likely heard of Anna Viola Pedersen, affectionately known as "Anna Pete." She went to Hinsdale when she was only 19 years old and worked at the hospital for 57 years. According to Sieberman, she loved to tell people, "I'm a Great Dane. I was born in Copenhagen!"

Whatever she did, noted Sieberman, Anna Pete did it well, whether it was in housekeeping, food service, laundry, or as an elevator operator. A good cook, she often prepared a midnight supper for the night staff, who especially liked her potato soup made with cream.

Anna Pete never married and had few relatives. She lived in a one-room apartment owned by the hospital. There she grew amaryllis plants, which she never kept for herself. Even in her advanced years when she could only walk with a cane, she personally delivered her amaryllis blooms to the hospital information desk for others to enjoy.

When she retired, well into her eighties, she feared having to move from the apartment, but the hospital allowed her to stay. Today the building in which she lived is called Anna Pedersen Hall in her honor. Seiberman recalled:

> *I saw that Anna Pete had her medicines and took care of her until she could no longer walk. At that point she was moved to a private home where she died in 1972 at age ninety-four. Anna Pete is buried in a hospital cemetery lot with twenty-four other former employees—only steps away from the graves of David and Mary Paulson, founders of the hospital where this Great Dane served for more than half a century.*

In 2014 Adventist Medical Center Hinsdale became part of AMITA Health, a joint operating company formed by Adventist Health System and Ascension Health. Today, the 276-bed facility remains the only teaching hospital in Dupage County, and it is recognized as a leader in a wide range of medical fields. As such, it continues to provide superior health care with Christian compassion to residents in the western suburbs of Chicago, just as Paulson prayed it would do.

SOURCES

Clough, Caroline Louise, *His Name was David*, Washington, D.C.: Review and Herald Publishing Association, 1955.

Dugan, Hugh G., *Hinsdale Sanitarium and Hospital 1904 to 1957*. (Publisher and date unknown.)

"Hinsdale Hospital: Weaving a Tapestry Through Ninety Years of Caring," *Visions*, Anniversary Issue, 1995.

Nelson, George, *The Kettering Medical Center: Recollections and Reflections of the Early Years*. 1996.

Paulson, David, *Footprints of Faith*, Hinsdale, Illinois: Life Boat Publishing Company, 1921.

Robinson, D.E., *The Story of Our Health Message*, Nashville, Tennessee: Southern Publishing Association, 1965.

Interviews: Ray Pelton and Katherine Sieberman.

Healthy Spot on God's Footstool

Washington Adventist Hospital: Takoma Park, Maryland | Founded 1907

Sometime in the 1880s, two community leaders walked across the undeveloped land above Sligo Creek in Takoma Park, Maryland. They noticed that the sound of water could be heard more clearly from one particular spot than from any other point on the property. One commented that "nature had designed this place" for a health care facility. Later a physician named Dr. Flower cleared part of the 50-acre site to build a medical institution. He invested about $60,000 in the project but never finished it.

Several years later leaders of the Seventh-day Adventist Church found this property not far from Washington, D.C. and bought it for only $6,000. The church established what is now known as Washington Adventist University on this property in 1904, but it would be three more years before a sanitarium opened there. In the meantime, from 1904 until 1914, the church operated a "Branch San" in the rented former residence of Ulysses S. Grant. Located in Washington, D.C. on what is now Logan Circle, its patrons included many government officials and their families.

Construction of a four-story structure with large verandahs finally began in Takoma Park in 1906. The following year the Washington Sanitarium and a school of nursing opened with Drs. Daniel and Lauretta Kress as the first medical director and chief surgeon, respectively. Dr. Daniel would serve as medical director from 1907 to 1909 and again from 1937 to 1938. Dr. Lauretta was the first licensed female physician in Montgomery County. While her primary role was as surgeon, she also headed the maternity department. During her 31 years at the Washington Sanitarium, she delivered more than 5,000 babies.

The Kresses had studied and worked at Battle Creek in the late 1800s, and between 1899 and 1907 they helped establish health care facilities in Great Britain, Australia, and New Zealand. In many ways the Washington Sanitarium was another mission field for them. As Dr. Daniel explained in an autobiography he co-authored with his wife, the San was in the country and accessible only by undeveloped roads. Although built to accommodate 35 patients, few people knew about the San, and often the staff outnumbered patients.

Life at the early Washington Sanitarium was typical of Adventist health centers of that time. Guests attended lectures, ate in the dining room, and worked in the sanitarium gardens. For recreation they exercised in the gymnasium and played croquet, shuffleboard, and golf. A sanitarium orchestra also frequently provided entertainment.

In those early days, the Washington Sanitarium may have been one of the best-kept secrets in the area. Those who patronized it spoke highly of the location and the care they received. Among those guests was the Superintendent of Government Gardens, who penned an article for the *Washington Star* newspaper applauding the facility and calling it "the healthiest spot on God's footstool." He wrote:

> *Seekers of the picturesque will be delighted with the scenes which present themselves in quick succession, along one of the most delightful rural drives through the healthiest region around Washington, in fact, not surpassed anywhere…God's great out-of-doors, combined with the rational treatments, the hygienic diet, and the spiritual atmosphere which pervades the institution, make this an ideal place for health seekers or for those who feel the need of an occasional period of rest and recreation.*

The Kresses devoted themselves to making the Washington Sanitarium succeed. For that to happen, two important things were needed—patients and money. When Dr. Harry Miller, a missionary physician and surgeon in China, returned to the United States in 1911 due to illness, church leaders asked him to head the Washington San. After he recovered, he assumed the dual position as medical director of the sanitarium and director of the denomination's worldwide medical work. He worked harmoniously alongside the Drs. Kress, having been previously acquainted with them. In fact, many years earlier, Dr. Daniel had encouraged him to study medicine at Battle Creek.

The San was still paying off its building debt when Miller arrived in 1913. The facility had just experienced a typhoid epidemic among the employees, which resulted in low patient admissions. Miller said patient rounds during his early days consisted primarily of shaking hands with three or four older women. In fact, to maintain his surgical skills, he reportedly opened an animal hospital on the back lawn of the sanitarium.

The financial situation began to improve after word spread that Miller had successfully performed a very difficult operation. He also did post-graduate work in thyroid surgery, and soon the San became a thriving thyroid center. The doctor donated his fees to the sanitarium, saving only enough to meet his personal expenses.

Business outgrew the original facility by 1916, and Miller recommended constructing a separate building for surgery. With the memory of high debt still in their minds, the board said no. Miller went ahead anyway, and by the time the board members learned of it, the roofers were already at work. Miller promised the building would be paid for within a year, but it actually opened debt-free—paid for primarily out of his fees from thyroid surgeries.

Patients began coming to the Washington Sanitarium from near and far. They represented many walks of life—from government officials and foreign diplomats to charity patients. Sometimes their stays at the San produced unexpected benefits for Adventist health care. For example, one patient told his family and friends about his experience at the Washington Sanitarium, and as a result, Drs. Miller and Kress were asked to help establish a sanitarium in Greeneville, Tennessee.

Miller remained in Takoma Park until he returned to China in 1925. The Kresses stayed until 1938. Dr. Daniel specialized in narcotics education and made a significant contribution to the field before he and Dr. Lauretta retired to Florida.

"God's great out-of-doors, combined with the rational treatments, the hygienic diet, and the spiritual atmosphere which pervades the institution, make this an ideal place for health seekers or for those who feel the need of an occasional period of rest and recreation."

– EARLY WASHINGTON SANITARIUM GUEST

Dr. Daniel once commented that it must have been "a source of the greatest satisfaction" for the founder of Takoma Park to know that the land he had judged to be ideal for a sanitarium had indeed proven to be so. Kress believed that the Washington Sanitarium had reached its full potential by 1932 when he made the following statement at the facility's 25th anniversary: "The institution has now reached its full growth, since there exists no expectation of enlarging it any further. We believe it to be sufficiently large to do its best work."

The future brought many changes the Kresses could never have imagined as the sanitarium grew into a modern acute-care hospital. The main entrance was moved in 1939 from the side facing Sligo Creek to the side facing the college. A six-story structure built in 1950 replaced the old buildings that had made up the main part of the hospital, leaving many to wonder how the San would ever pay for its "extravagant" $1.4 million facility.

Among other developments, the 1960s saw the addition of an intensive-care unit, a school of X-ray technology, a school of practical nursing, an alcohol treatment center, and a coronary-care unit. Also during this time Chaplain Alfred Marple brought to Washington the "Five-Day Plan to Stop Smoking." During his 35 years at the hospital, he personally helped more than 50,000 people complete the smoking cessation program. In addition to offering classes at the hospital, he took the plan to various government offices in Washington, D.C.

The sanitarium's name was changed to Washington Adventist Hospital in the early 1970s, and a $12.5 million expansion increased the patient bed capacity to 366. Although the hospital later reduced the number of patient beds to 300, construction and growth continued throughout the 1990s.

While some worried about the increasing costs associated with expansion, it was a demolition project that generated the loudest outcry from the local community and church members. The original 1907 sanitarium building—a stately old structure that had been a landmark in Takoma Park for most of a century—did not meet fire and safety codes and was condemned for patient use.

Additionally, the cost of heating and cooling the structure was excessive, as was the cost of maintaining the old wood and stucco building. Hospital leaders figured it would take $1.2 million to renovate the building, a cost that would have to be passed on to patients, and even then the facility would remain inadequate. So, amid voices of protest, the building was demolished in 1982.

Guests attended lectures, ate in the dining room, and worked in the sanitarium gardens. For recreation they exercised in the gymnasium and played croquet, shuffleboard, and golf. A sanitarium orchestra also frequently provided entertainment.

In December 2015, Adventist HealthCare received approval to relocate Washington Adventist Hospital to the White Oak/Calverton area in the eastern area of Montgomery County. The move will not only expand access to care, but will also strengthen the collaborative partnership between Washington Adventist Hospital and the Food and Drug Administration. The new hospital is expected to open in 2019.

Washington Adventist Hospital remains the oldest operating hospital in Montgomery County, Maryland. While the peaceful, rural setting of the original facility continues to give way to modern urbanization, the hospital maintains the mission on which it was founded nearly a century ago— to meet the physical, mental, and spiritual needs of all those who come seeking care.

SOURCES

Jepson, Robert E., "A.C. Marple Kicks the Habit," *Visitor*, September 1, 1955.

Kress, Daniel and Lauretta, *Under the Guiding Hand*, Washington, D.C.: College Press, 1941.

Moore, Raymond S., *China Doctor, The Life Story of Harry Willis Miller*. Mt. View, California: Pacific Press Publishing Association, 1969.

"90 Years of Progress Spring from a Mission of Caring," 1979.

"Ten Years! Shady Grove Celebrates a Decade of Great Beginnings," *Evergreen*, Winter 1989.

Interviews and Notes: William Murrill.

Rocky Venture on the Cumberland

Tennessee Christian Medical Center | 1907–2006

The earliest Adventist medical work around Nashville began in the late 1890s with small treatment rooms offering massage and hydrotherapy services. But it wasn't until a self-supporting school and sanitarium were established in nearby Madison that the church's medical work gained solid footing in Tennessee.

Edward Sutherland and Percy Magan, teachers at Emmanuel Missionary College (today's Andrews University) in southwest Michigan, dreamed of establishing a school in the hills of Tennessee or the Carolinas where students would learn practical trades and simple medical treatments—a dream shared by Ellen G. White. With this in mind, Sutherland and Magan moved to Tennessee in 1904. Soon after their arrival, they were invited by Mrs. White to join her and a small group traveling up the Cumberland River on a boat called *Morning Star* operated by her son Edson White. The purpose of the trip was to look for suitable property for a school.

As it turned out, the boat broke down near an old plantation farm just a few miles outside of Nashville. While waiting for repairs, Mrs. White went ashore to explore the rock-covered, run-down property that had once been a slave-trading center. She returned to the boat and announced this was the place Magan and Sutherland should establish their school. The men adamantly disagreed.

> "Do you think I'd let the devil beat me out of a place for a thousand dollars? Pay the extra thousand. It's cheap enough."
>
> – ELLEN G. WHITE

"It's the roughest, weediest, most miserable thing I've ever seen," Sutherland told Magan. But Ellen G. White insisted it was the place God wanted them to build a school, and it was hard to quarrel with Mrs. White.

The two men sat down on one of the many rocks that populated the barren farm and cried over the seemingly impossible situation.

"It does me up and makes me sick, the whole thought of it," Sutherland said. "I wish we had some honorable and Christian way to get out of the whole thing without showing a lack of faith in the testimonies from the Lord's messenger."

The two men knelt and prayed, and then went home. The next day, they returned to the same rock and prayed once more, begging God to show them His will. This time their fears subsided, and God's answer seemed crystal clear. They must buy the property.

While Magan remained in Nashville to work out the purchase, Sutherland went to Michigan to see his widowed Aunt Nellie Druillard, hoping she would help them buy the Tennessee farm and establish the school. A woman of unusual business skill, Druillard was treasurer of Emmanuel Missionary College at that time. Many years earlier, she had sold some land for a large amount of money, and had generously used her wealth to support the church's health and education work.

When Sutherland told her about the farm, she thought it sounded like a "rocky" venture, to say the least. By this time, however, Sutherland was so convinced that the Lord had led them to that particular property that he told her he would find money elsewhere if she would not help. At last she agreed to go to Nashville to explore the idea.

Mrs. White was in Madison when Sutherland returned with his aunt. They soon learned that Magan had run into problems with the property owner's wife, who declared she would never sell to a Yankee. Although she finally relented and agreed to sell them the property, she increased the price by $1,000. Mrs. Druillard and Mrs. White reacted quite differently.

"Ha!" Mrs. Druillard exclaimed. "I'm glad we're not going to take it."

"Glad?!" Mrs. White's voice rang out. "'Glad?! Do you think I'd let the devil beat me out of a place for a thousand dollars? Pay the extra thousand. It's cheap enough."

Soon after the school opened, which later became known as Madison College, a sick man arrived and insisted that he would recover if given proper rest, a healthy diet, and the treatments they could provide. Although the school was not set up to take in patients, Mrs. Druillard hung a curtain on one end of a porch on the plantation house to make a room for him. After he recovered, he told others about his experience, and demand for medical care at Madison began to grow.

Madison was devoted to preparing students to work in rural areas where people suffered from poor health, inadequate educational facilities, and depleted agricultural land. At one time, there would be nearly fifty sites called "rural units" where Madison students and graduates provided health and educational services across Tennessee, Georgia, Mississippi, Alabama, Kentucky, and North Carolina.

While the original plan was to operate a sanitarium alongside the Madison school, there was hardly enough money to cover school needs, let alone medical work. Besides, neither Sutherland nor Magan had any experience running medical institutions. But once again, Mrs. White was full of ideas.

On a visit to Madison in 1906, she joined some students and faculty for a picnic. Enjoying the pleasant afternoon, she looked across the campus and announced, "This would be a good spot for a sanitarium." The response of the other picnickers was less than enthusiastic, but Mrs. White meant what she said.

"Get your people together, get a horse, and mark out the site, even though you don't have money to begin," she said.

After lunch and a brief prayer meeting, someone hitched a mule to a plow and marked out the spot as she had told them to do. The first medical building opened on that spot in 1908. It was a small cottage with 11 beds and treatment rooms, lighted by kerosene lamps, and equipped with a wood stove and a treatment table made out of a wide board placed across two wooden sawhorses.

Finances continued to be an issue for the school and sanitarium. As a self-supporting organization, it received little denominational assistance. To complicate matters, Madison leaders were notified in 1911 that they could no longer publish fundraising articles or report school and sanitarium activities in the church paper, *The Review and Herald.*

Fortunately, in addition to Mrs. Druillard, Madison attracted the attention of two other wealthy widows, Josephine Gotzian and Lida Funk Scott, daughter of Wilfred Funk of the Funk and Wagnall Publishing Company. These women donated thousands of dollars to Madison as well as other early Adventist healthcare ventures.

Magan's wife, Lillian, was Madison's first staff physician, but the facility desperately needed more doctors. Dr. Newton Evans, who assisted for a time, eventually moved to the new Adventist medical school in California, the College of Medical Evangelists. Finally, at the ages of 46 and 42 respectively, Sutherland and Magan enrolled in the University of Tennessee Medical School in Nashville. They graduated in 1914, planning to strengthen the medical program at Madison. However, the very next year brought an unexpected turn of events.

Dr. Evans persuaded Magan to join him in California to develop a clinical program for the church's fledgling medical school. It was a difficult separation for Magan and Sutherland, who had worked together for many years. After Magan became dean of the medical school, other Madison staff joined him in California, but Sutherland remained at Madison the rest of his life. Though separated by miles, the two men remained close friends and confidants.

For instance, when Magan realized the medical school needed a hospital in Los Angeles to provide a clinical training site for future doctors, he turned to Sutherland for financial support, and his friend came through for him. It just so happened that Lida Scott Funk had recently promised a substantial gift to Madison for much-needed improvements. When Sutherland presented her with the problems of the medical school in California, she agreed to send $30,000 to Magan. Eventually Madison increased the gift to $50,000.

Madison College and Madison Hospital transferred to denominational ownership in 1963, and the college closed in 1964. The following year the old sanitarium buildings were razed and a replacement facility built that eventually increased the hospital's bed capacity to 311. The name was changed to Tennessee Christian Medical Center in 1985. In addition, a 50-bed sister facility known as Highland Hospital—established as Fountain Head Sanitarium in 1929—in nearby Portland, became a satellite hospital in 1994. It was renamed Tennessee Christian Medical Center-Portland. In 2006, Hospital Corporation of American acquired the two facilities from Adventist Health Systems.

SOURCES

Gish, Ira and Harry Christman, *Madison—God's Beautiful Farm: The E. A. Sutherland Story*, Nampa, Idaho: The Upward Way, 1989.

Hansen, Louis A., *From So Small a Dream*, Nashville: Southern Publishing Association, 1968.

Rittenhouse, Floyd O. Rittenhouse, "E.A. Sutherland, Independent Reformer," *Adventist Heritage*, Winter 1977. *Madison College: School of Divine Origin 1904-1964,* Madison College Alumni Association, 1986.

Bryant, Paul A., Komala Dewantara, Eduardo A. Gonzalez, Carol Grannon, Ulrike Hasel, Christina Maria O. Matos, Kenneth E. McHenry, Erling B. Snorrason, Carol Williams; Jerry Moon, instructor, editor, *Edward Alexander Sutherland and Madison College, 1904-1964*, Berrien Springs, Michigan: Andrews University School of Education, 1989.

Parmele's $9,000 Success Story

Florida Hospital: Orlando, Florida | Founded 1908

Soon after Rufus Wells Parmele moved to Florida in 1907, he began looking for a place to open a health center similar to the Adventist facilities that now stretched across the United States and overseas. Coming from Nashville, Parmele and his physician wife, Lydia, were well acquainted with the church's early medical work. Before completing her medical training, Lydia had worked as a nurse with her parents in Vicksburg, Mississippi. She was also familiar with Riverside Hospital and the Madison Sanitarium in Tennessee.

The Parmeles found an abandoned tuberculosis facility that had been developed by a Dr. R.L. Harris at a cost of more than $12,000. Located on 72 acres, the lakeside property included a large frame building, four cottages, and a dairy herd. Trees, orange groves, flowering shrubbery, and palms enhanced the peaceful setting. Parmele, president of the newly organized Florida Conference of Seventh-day Adventists, offered $9,000 for the property, although the conference had only $4.83 on its books.

When the owner accepted his offer, Parmele turned to local church members to raise the purchase money. They welcomed the opportunity to begin a Battle Creek-style medical facility in Central Florida and quickly raised enough money through contributions and stock purchases to avoid incurring debt. Adventist health pioneer Ellen G. White was nothing but supportive:

"I have no hesitancy in saying that I believe the time has come for Florida to have a sanitarium, so that the light which our sanitariums are established to reflect may shine forth to the people of Florida and to the many health seekers who come from the northern states."

The 20-bed Florida Sanitarium opened in October, 1908, with two physicians, four patients, a nurse, and a few other workers. In time, Parmele's $9,000 investment would reap a healthy return for Adventist health care, but early growth was hampered by dramatic seasonal fluctuations in population. Florida attracted many wealthy "snowbirds" from the northern states who enjoyed a spa-like winter vacation at the sanitarium, availing themselves of hydrotherapy treatments, massages, a healthful diet, and recreation. While blizzards blew up North, sanitarium guests spent pleasant winter days in Florida playing croquet, shuffleboard, tennis, and golf; watching water birds and alligators in the nearby lake; or relaxing in rocking chairs on the broad porches overlooking Lake Estelle. When winter passed they returned to their northern homes, fleeing the Sunshine State's steamy summers. Yet business was not limited to the resort-type resident. From the beginning, doctors provided acute-care services ranging from surgery to maternity care.

Most organizations experience personnel conflicts of one sort or another, and the young Florida San was no exception. According to author Louis Hansen in *From So Small A Dream*, a serious rift developed between the business manager and medical director around 1929. Among other things, in an effort to avoid malpractice lawsuits, the business manager insisted on being present for all surgeries, which infuriated the physicians. It became virtually impossible to attract new physicians, and it took several years and personnel changes to remedy the situation.

In the days before air conditioning, summers presented special challenges for the surgical staff. As explained in *Through the Years*, published in 1998 for the hospital's 90th anniversary, "…ceiling and wall-mounted fans provided the only source of cooling…. The surgery rooms were particularly sweltering—the hot surgical lights created immense heat, and the rooms could not be cooled by fans or other devices which might spread dust or particles." Air conditioning was finally installed in 1958.

Not all Floridians were immediate fans of the facility. In the early 1950s, Martin Andersen was not impressed with the Florida Sanitarium and Hospital. As editor, and later owner and publisher, of *The Orlando Sentinel*, he refused to print anything about the hospital in the newspaper.

Homer Grove, the hospital's public relations director at the time, arranged for Andersen to receive free physical therapy treatments. Andersen accepted the invitation, and in time came to appreciate the hospital staff. After a while he began bringing them copies of the newspaper and also gave orchids to new mothers. He sometimes invited his therapist to vacation at his beach house. And, eventually, he told Grove he would print whatever he gave to the newspaper. This went on for more than 10 years. Andersen even arranged to build a house on hospital property so he could live there in his final years.

Over time he and his wife Gracia generously donated millions of dollars to the hospital, and a number of facilities are named in their honor, including a garden and orchid room, the Martin

Andersen wing at Florida Hospital Orlando, and the Martin Andersen Cancer Center at Florida Hospital Altamonte.

With the 1960s came an important period in the history of Central Florida—and consequently for Adventist health care. These were boom years for tourism and business, and under Don Welch's administration from 1961 to 1973, the hospital made its final transition from a sanitarium to a modern acute-care facility.

> "I have no hesitancy in saying that I believe the time has come for Florida to have a sanitarium, so that the light which our sanitariums are established to reflect may shine forth to the people of Florida and to the many health seekers who come from the northern states."
>
> – ELLEN G. WHITE

One of Welch's first challenges was a medical staff that had little interest in growing in either quality or quantity. Welch believed that Adventist health care had the opportunity to improve its mission of quality care and service in Central Florida. It could become a leader—or risk being left behind while other hospitals marched in step with the rapidly growing community. As a result, the 34-year-old administrator took some tough stands to upgrade the staff and attract additional board-certified physicians.

Big changes were occurring in the health care industry, and the timing was right for Florida Hospital. During the Welch years the hospital grew from 160 to 474 patient beds, and initiated such services and programs as the region's first intensive-care unit, a cardiac-care unit that provided cardiac catheterization and open-heart surgery, the nation's first orthopedic "clean air surgery," a family practice residency program, and an organ transplant program. Welch also bought a large pasture north of Orlando and, in 1973, opened a 104-bed satellite facility called Florida Hospital Altamonte. Today the hospital maintains 278 beds.

From time to time, Florida Hospital received requests to open hospitals in other communities or to manage existing hospitals. But there was no organizational mechanism for such arrangements. As they watched the changes occurring throughout the health care industry, however, Welch and other Adventist leaders recognized that, if they were to survive, the church's many small, stand-alone hospitals would have to become part of larger systems that could provide strong management expertise, centralization of certain services, and the benefits of economies of scale. With this in mind, Welch left Florida Hospital in 1973 to devote his attention to pioneering the organization that is today's Adventist Health System.

Bob Scott followed Welch as president of Florida Hospital, and it continued to flourish under his direction. During this time, the 50-bed hospital in Apopka, a town north of Orlando, became the second Florida Hospital satellite.

Mardian Blair came from Portland Adventist Hospital and the Northwest Medical Foundation in Oregon to serve as Florida Hospital president from 1979 to 1984. He had begun his health care career in 1958 at Hinsdale. During his time there and then at Portland, he demonstrated a skill to move health care facilities to the next level. Florida Hospital was no exception. Among other advances, he oversaw the development of the Florida Heart Institute and a $120 million construction project that included a medical office building, a freestanding psychiatric center, and a patient tower that increased the Orlando facility's capacity to 849 beds.

In 1984 Welch was appointed president of what turned out to be the short-lived national Adventist health system. Blair was named president of what was then called Adventist Health System/Sunbelt, consisting of the Adventist hospitals in the southern and southwestern U.S.

Tom Werner took over the helm of Florida Hospital in 1984 and led the organization through the next 16 years of growth, innovation, and expanded services. Centers of excellence were developed in such areas as cancer treatment, women's medicine, orthopedics, neurology and more. Relationships with community-based organizations, including Disney, the Orlando Magic and others, led to cooperative projects that continued to strengthen the Adventist hospital's presence throughout Central Florida. Also a new college for health sciences offered convenient educational opportunities on the Orlando campus.

In the developing years of Adventist Health System, Florida Hospital had supported many of the church's hospitals in the southern and southwestern United States until they either became financially viable or were divested. At the same time, opportunities came for the flagship hospital to enlarge its service area in Central Florida.

The concept of satellite hospitals envisioned by Welch in the 1970s continued through the next four decades under the leadership of Don Jernigan, Lars Houmann and Daryl Tol as many stand-alone hospitals sought to unite with a successful not-for-profit organization that would ensure continued quality health care services to their communities.

Little did Parmele know a $9,000 investment in an old TB sanatorium in 1908 would one day grow into the multi-campus organization that is Florida Hospital today. With 25 facilities stretching across the Sunshine State from Daytona Beach to Tampa Bay, the Florida Hospital division of Adventist Health System serves more than one million patients per year, and in 2015 provided more than 129 million in charity care.

With God's blessing, Florida Hospital continues to extend the healing ministry of Christ—reflecting His light to the people in Florida and beyond.

SOURCES

"Florida Hospital: 75 Years of Care. 75 Years of Caring," 1983.

Hansen, Louis A., *From So Small a Dream*, Nashville, Tennessee: Southern Publishing Association, 1968.

Norman, R. Steven III, "Edson White's Southern Work Remembered," *Southern Tidings*, February 2001.

Howes, Melinda, *Florida Hospital: Through the Years*, Orlando, Florida: Florida Hospital, 1998.

Interviews and Notes: Rich Rainer and William Murrill.

The Lord Would Be Pleased

Park Ridge Health: Fletcher, North Carolina | Founded 1910

Adventist health care in North Carolina began with a conversation between two women near Asheville one evening in 1909. Ellen G. White had stopped in town while traveling by train from Tennessee to a meeting of church leaders in Washington, D.C. Ever since the end of the Civil War, she had urged farmers, builders, teachers, and missionaries to move to the South, but few had responded.

After speaking to a group of church members in Asheville, Mrs. White stayed in the home of Martha Rumbough. The wife of an inventor and daughter of a manufacturer, Rumbough had generously shared her wealth to help establish churches in the region. On that evening in 1909 she mentioned that she would like to do more for God's Kingdom. Mrs. White was ready for her offer.

"The Lord would be pleased if you would start a medical and educational work in the vicinity of Asheville," she said.

Two local men also played an important part in establishing a school and medical facility in this area. One was Arthur Whitefield Spalding, an author and teacher formerly from Emmanuel Missionary College (Today's Andrews University) in Michigan. He was writing and selling books, trying to recruit others to western North Carolina. The second man was Professor Sidney Brownsberger, a teacher, administrator, and minister. He had purchased a small farm where he and his wife lived with their three children.

Spalding took on the responsibility of finding a suitable location for the proposed project. Mrs. White had specified a country setting with a good supply of water and timber, available soil, access to roads and railways, and buildings on the property. While selling books one day, he learned of a rundown place known as Byers' Plantation, and he set out to find it. The book *Mountain Memories* describes his first impressions:

> *The road was winding and dusty and long until he topped a hill. He stood where the road crossed the old Indian trading path known as the Howard Gap Road, and looked down into a valley…. [The old plantation] had been worked since 1798. The topsoil had eroded, and deep red gullies ribboned the area near the dilapidated old barn. The two-story farmhouse dated from 1885 and was in great need of repairs. Weeds and brush were everywhere. But into Spalding's poetic mind came recollections of the words, 'As the mountains are round about Jerusalem' (Psalm 125:2), and he knew this was the place he was searching for.*

According to the deed dated March 11, 1910, the Adventists purchased 416 acres for $5,750. The trustees named in the deed were Martha E. Rumbough, Edward A. Sutherland, R.L. Williams, Percy T. Magan, and Sidney Brownsberger. This was the beginning of Fletcher Academy and Park Ridge Health. With the construction of a cottage that housed two treatment rooms in 1916, Adventists built the first health care facility for the mountain people of western North Carolina, which was for many years known as the Mountain Sanitarium. In the early days patients came by horse and buggy or wagon, and later by train. They stayed in individual cottages where meals and medications were delivered to them. Sometime in 1927 a larger building was completed with a long porch where patients could enjoy the peaceful views and surroundings of the Blue Ridge Mountains. The sanitarium also operated a school of nursing for 56 years. Its graduates were highly sought after by hospitals all over the country as well as for overseas service.

> With the construction of a cottage that housed two treatment rooms in 1916, Adventists built the first health care facility for the mountain people of western North Carolina, which was for many years known as the Mountain Sanitarium.

Brownsberger's son and daughter, John and Ethel Brownsberger, both Madison College graduates, were the first nurses at the Mountain San and the first registered nurses in North Carolina. In 1920 John married Elsie Peterson, a young woman he had proposed to at Madison College in 1914. Amazingly, they had seen each other only twice during the six years that lapsed between the proposal and the wedding. John and another nurse, Forrest Bliss, studied medicine at the College of Medical Evangelists in California and returned to work at the Mountain San after completing their education.

The authors of *Mountain Memories* recounted the Brownsberger's dedicated service:

> *After the untimely death of two daughters in 1929, John and Elsie buried themselves in the work of developing the Hospital and School of Nursing at Fletcher. John worked untiringly during the depression years, many times getting paid in farm produce or labor, as money was scarce. He often would be called out at night to travel over muddy mountain roads to see patients. He never complained except once when he arrived at a remote farmhouse at 2 a.m. to discover that his patient was a sick cow! He did all types of surgery during those years and obstetrics—many times giving the anesthetic as well. It was during this time that he helped to establish the Blue Shield Insurance Plan for North Carolina....*

✳

Another name closely linked to the history of the Mountain San is Lelia Patterson, who devoted her life to the health needs of the mountain people. A registered nurse from the Hinsdale Sanitarium near Chicago, she moved to Asheville in 1919 to help start a vegetarian cafeteria and treatment room. That facility, called Good Health Place, merged with the Mountain San in 1920, and Patterson began a 43-year affiliation with the hospital.

When she died in 1975, Leila Patterson left a legacy of compassionate care and a pioneering spirit that was the hallmark of many early Adventist health care workers.

Her services were available to all regardless of color, creed, or ability to pay. She took food and clothing to those in need and used her own money to help pay their hospital bills. Through her Good Neighbor Clubs, she taught people how to grow their own food, prepare nutritious meals, and improve family health.

In the early days she traveled by Model-T Ford over unpaved mountain roads around Asheville to treat the sick and deliver babies. Her services were available to all regardless of color, creed, or ability to pay. She took food and clothing to those in need and used her own money to help pay their hospital bills. Through her Good Neighbor Clubs, she taught people how to grow their own food, prepare nutritious meals, and improve family health.

The name of the Mountain San was changed to Fletcher Hospital around 1973. It became part of Adventist Health System/Sunbelt Health Care Corporation in 1984. The name was changed to Park Ridge Hospital in 1985, and the present facility opened in 1986. The former hospital building now houses a long-term-care facility operated by Adventist Care Centers, a division of Adventist Health System. After more than 100 years, Park Ridge Health, as it is known today, still provides an environment of Christian compassion and care for those in need of healing, health, or hope.

SOURCES

Mountain Memories—The Story of Mountain Sanitarium and Hospital School of Nursing, Collegedale, Tennessee: The College Press, undated.

"Lelia Patterson Center: Doorway to Lifestyle Enhancement," (fundraising publication), Fletcher, North Carolina: Fletcher Academy, undated.

Training Center in the City

White Memorial Medical Center: Los Angeles, California | Founded 1913

A gentle knock interrupted a crucial meeting of church officials and leaders of the College of Medical Evangelists at Loma Linda, California, in 1915. Despite all the hard work of school leaders, the school had received only a C rating—the lowest possible—from the American Medical Association's accrediting agency. The men had gathered to decide the future of the young school. Who would dare interrupt such an important meeting?

The door opened upon four women who asked to enter the room: Josephine Gotzian, a woman of means who had contributed generously to the Madison Sanitarium and Hospital, the Paradise Valley Sanitarium, the Portland Sanitarium and Hospital, and other facilities; Hetty Haskell, a teacher and wife of the popular evangelist Stephen Haskell who was known for her faith and belief in the power of the Word of God; her widowed sister, Emma Gray, a person with more faith than money, but with a history of overcoming great obstacles; and Dr. Florence Keller, a physician from the Glendale Sanitarium who had served with her husband in New Zealand.

> In addition to working in the clinic, student nurses and medical students also made "home deliveries" throughout East Los Angeles. This was called "Outside OB" and often required middle-of-the-night trips by streetcar to help women deliver their babies at home.

These women—sent by Dr. Percy Magan's friend, Dr. Edward Sutherland in Tennessee—had something to say about the College of Medical Evangelists. They asked that the school be allowed to continue, and that a teaching hospital be built in Los Angeles to house the clinical division. Further, they suggested that the hospital should be dedicated to the memory of Ellen G. White, who had recently died. The men were not to worry about the money for the hospital, but were to leave that in the hands of the women of the church.

Needless to say, the men were speechless. Magan later said a "sacred hush pervaded the room" as the women thanked the men for their courtesy and left.

The White Memorial Medical Center had begun as an outpatient clinic in 1913 to provide clinical experience for students at the College of Medical Evangelists, now Loma Linda University School of Medicine. After receiving the dismal accreditation rating, some thought the time had come to close the school, but others believed Adventists were called to a medical mission requiring fully qualified physicians. After the ladies' passionate plea at the meeting, the vote was taken to continue the four-year program and build a teaching facility in Los Angeles.

The school bought a block of property in the Boyle Heights area near the Los Angeles County Hospital where medical students were already receiving some of their clinical training. The first cottages making up the new White Memorial Hospital opened in January 1918, with additional bungalows being built as money became available. Eventually, "The White," as it became known, consisted of nine buildings filling the entire block.

Hectic workdays in Los Angeles were a sharp contrast to the tranquil sanitarium life in rural Loma Linda. In the first 10 years of operation, the clinic averaged 71,000 patients per year, more than any other outpatient facility in the city. The White provided a large amount of charity care funded largely through contracts with a railroad company, the Los Angeles police and fire departments, and the Ascot Speedway.

In addition to working in the clinic, student nurses and medical students also made "home deliveries" throughout East Los Angeles. This was called "Outside OB" and often required middle-of-the-night trips by streetcar to help women deliver their babies at home. These experiences produced many interesting stories, some of which may have strayed slightly from the truth as they were told and retold over the years. Maxine Atteberry related the following in her history of the Loma Linda University School of Nursing:

> *An inept medical student had delivered his first baby. When he tried to lift the infant by the feet as he had seen done, the baby slipped through his fingers and fell to the floor. He picked him up, fortunately unhurt and squalling lustily. When he looked up he was facing the disapproving eyes of the baby's grandmother. Having a presence of mind which far exceeded his manual dexterity, he quickly said, 'He's a fine baby, Ma'am. We sometimes have to drop 'em two or three times to make 'em cry.'*

Erwin Remboldt was the White's administrator/president for 10 years. He arrived in 1950 after graduating from Union College in Lincoln, Nebraska. With his new business degree, he expected to get "a fairly reasonable job." Instead, he had to get up at 5 a.m. to post the patient ledger.

"I didn't even know how to run an adding machine," he said.

After a few months he was appointed assistant accountant and was later named personnel director. Then one day the dean at Loma Linda offered to send him to school for an advanced degree in hospital administration. After graduating he returned and provided leadership until 1960 when he went to Glendale. Within four years Remboldt would be administrator of both facilities.

Hectic workdays in Los Angeles were a sharp contrast to the tranquil sanitarium life in rural Loma Linda. In the first 10 years of operation, the clinic averaged 71,000 patients per year, more than any other outpatient facility in the city.

When the medical school moved its clinical division to Loma Linda in 1964, Remboldt was asked to serve also as administrator of White Memorial, which was in financial trouble. It was located in a low-income part of Los Angeles, the medical staff needed reorganizing, and two floors had been closed due of a lack of nurses. Remboldt and his administrative team spent a lot of time on their knees, praying that the Lord would help them find personnel. After about four months enough nurses were found to staff the vacant floors.

Every week it seemed that a physician or key employee moved away from The White to Loma Linda. Fortunately, the remaining medical staff rallied to support the needs of the local community and turn the place around. Among other actions, this recovery meant eliminating the partial pay operation of the clinic, which gave patients the option of not paying part of their bills based on their circumstances.

The facility has faced multiple challenges over the years, but none more critical than a financial crisis in the late 1980s created by an increasing number of Medi-Cal and indigent patients, which threatened to end the hospital's long history of service in East Los Angeles. Frank Dupper, then president of Adventist Health, recalled the experience:

> A consultant I had known when he headed Medi-Cal called to tell me California Senate Bill 855 was within days of coming up for a vote. It meant millions of state and federal dollars for government teaching hospitals and children's hospitals that care for a high number of Medi-Cal and indigent patients. With only some minor modifications, it could include some other hospitals that met certain qualifications for these disproportional share funds. He said it could mean $10 million for more a year for White Memorial.

> Harvey Rudisaile, then president of The White, went to see officials at the Los Angeles County Hospital who were spearheading the bill, and in no time enlisted their support for changing the bill.

> Meanwhile, I telephoned a prominent attorney in Los Angeles who agreed to work with us. Then I called my friends at the Catholic and Lutheran hospitals in Los Angeles, as well as the California Healthcare Association. Miraculously, I reached all of these individuals on my first call. Within a couple of days, changes were made to widen the net of hospitals eligible for these funds. The bill passed with our changes, literally saving The White from closure and allowing it to continue serving the people of East Los Angeles.

SOURCES

Atteberry, Maxine, *From Pinafores to Pantsuits*: *The Story of Loma Linda University School of Nursing*, Loma Linda, California, 1975.

Graybill, Ronald D, *A Journey of Faith and Healing*, White Memorial Medical Center, 2013.

Herber, Raymond, editor, *The Department of Medicine from 1909 to 2000*, Loma Linda, California: Department of Medicine, School of Medicine of Loma Linda University, 1999.

Johns, Warren L., and Richard H. Utt, editors, *The Vision Bold*, Washington, D.C.: Review and Herald Publishing Association, 1977.

Judd, Wayne, tape recorded interviews with Don Ammon, Frank Dupper and Erwin Remboldt, 1998.

Interviews: Frank Dupper, Ray Pelton and Erwin Remboldt.

Influence of a Surgeon's Prayer

Takoma Regional Hospital: Greeneville, Tennessee | Founded 1928

In the early 1920s, some affluent patients from Greene County, Tennessee, went to the Washington San in Takoma Park, Maryland, for health care services. They had learned about the facility through one of Dr. Harry Miller's former patients. This man had been extremely depressed and was considering suicide when Miller told him he needed a portion of his colon removed. Figuring he would never live through surgery, the man agreed to the operation.

Miller offered his usual prayer before surgery, unaware that the patient expected to die. As it turned out, the man not only recovered, but his whole outlook on life changed—largely as a result of hearing the physician's prayer. Feeling better than ever, the man told his family and friends back in Tennessee about his experience, and they also started going to the Washington San. Eventually, someone spoke with Miller and his colleague, Dr. Daniel Kress, about opening a sanitarium in Greeneville.

Miller and Kress had both been pioneer missionaries—Miller in China, and Kress with his physician wife Lauretta in England, Australia, and New Zealand. The two men traveled to Tennessee and were duly impressed with the quiet community in Greene County. But the people would have to wait for a man named Coolidge to bring them a sanitarium.

After working six years in a Pennsylvania mining community, a young Dr. LeRoy Coolidge realized that he was not living the life he wanted. He moved to Washington, D.C., where he had attended medical school, and joined the staff of the Washington Sanitarium. There he worked with Dr. Miller, who had a profound influence on him.

Meanwhile back in Greeneville, local resident Roy Bowen and his wife, both graduate nurses, set up hydrotherapy rooms and a vegetarian cafeteria in a large house on Main Street in 1923. Miller and Coolidge went there three times in 1925 to perform surgeries. Coolidge finally moved to Greeneville and in 1926 bought the small facility, which was renamed the Branch Takoma Park Sanitarium. Two registered nurses from the Washington San came to help him.

Another nurse, Virgil Robert Bottomley, also from the Washington San, was Coolidge's right-hand man from 1926 to 1941, doing just about anything that needed to be done, from bookkeeping to X-rays. At age 41, he enrolled in medical school at the University of Tennessee at Memphis. After graduating, he returned to Greeneville, where he admitted patients to Takoma Hospital for many years.

A school of nursing was started in 1926. Interestingly, the student uniforms were modeled after those used at Walter Reed Army Hospital where Coolidge's sisters studied in Washington, D.C. The Takoma school trained registered nurses for 20 years. It became a practical nursing program in 1946, and at one time offered a "missionary nurse" course. Coolidge considered nursing to be "a profession based on sacrifice and service," and he was pleased that many Takoma graduates became overseas missionaries.

When the Main Street facility became inadequate, 24 community leaders organized a corporation and invested at least $1,000 each. One person donated land to build a three-story, 40-bed hospital, which opened on January 1, 1928. Coolidge gradually bought out the stockholders, and in 1954 deeded the hospital to the Southern Union Conference of Seventh-day Adventists.

As founder, owner, and medical director, Coolidge had the first and last word regarding the hospital as long as he was associated with it. He even helped choose his successor, Dr. James Ray McKinney.

After finishing an internship at White Memorial Hospital in Los Angeles in 1960, Dr. McKinney went home to Morristown, Tennessee for a little vacation before returning for a surgical residency. One day while there, R.E. Crawford from the Georgia-Cumberland Conference of Seventh-day Adventists came to see him.

"Dr. Coolidge is 71 years old, and he's sitting up there in Greeneville with no help. That's why I've come to see you—to ask you to go up there and work with him at Takoma Hospital," Crawford said.

"I can't do that," McKinney replied. "I'm going back to California."

Crawford begged the young man to drive 30 miles to Greeneville and just talk with Coolidge, which McKinney finally agreed to do. He knew Coolidge was a good surgeon—a Fellow in the

American College of Surgeons and in the International College of Surgeons. When he was a boy, McKinney's mother had taken him to see Coolidge.

The older doctor explained how he had started the hospital in the 1920s and in 1960 was still captain of the ship. However, he said, the time had come to turn it over to a younger person. Coolidge asked McKinney to do the job for one year. Twenty-six-year-old McKinney joined him in 1960, and that one-year trial turned into a career lasting more than 41 years.

"He kind of adopted me as his son," said McKinney. "For 10 years I stood under him, and he taught me surgery."

The young doctor knew if the hospital was to be successful, some changes must be made. The physical facility was outdated, and no diagnostic work was happening in X-ray or lab.

"I called Don Rees, president of the Southern Union, and told him, 'You've got to send me some help if I'm going to make this place survive,'" McKinney recalled.

Rees asked Don Welch, the new administrator at the Florida Sanitarium and Hospital in Orlando, to go to Greeneville and see what he could do. Although Welch and McKinney were both from Tennessee, they had never met. McKinney recalled:

> *Don came up, we formed a finance committee, and we started spending money. We upgraded the facility. We put in new lighting. We put in a new entrance. We put in new carpet. We bought new laboratory equipment and hired new staff. Don came once every three months for about five years. He had grown up at Madison, which was based on the idea of a large hospital helping all these little hospitals. So, at the same time he was building up Florida Hospital, he started helping in other places, and he began to see that a health system would benefit the church's hospitals.*

Years later, while attending an Annual Council of Adventist church leaders in the early 1970s, McKinney watched Welch writing names on the back of an envelope.

"I'm forming a new board, and I think you could help," Welch said.

"Well, Don, if you think I could help, I'd be happy to do it," McKinney said.

The list on the envelope was the beginning of the first board of directors for the Adventist Health System/Sunbelt Healthcare Corporation, formed in 1973. Takoma Regional Hospital was among the church-operated facilities that became part of that organization. McKinney served on the board until April 2001. He was also on the board of Adventist Health System/US during the four years it existed, 1985-1989.

Miller offered his usual prayer before surgery, unaware that the patient expected to die. As it turned out, the man not only recovered, but his whole outlook on life changed—largely as a result of hearing the physician's prayer. Feeling better than ever, the man told his family and friends back in Tennessee about his experience, and they also started going to the Washington San.

After seven years at Takoma, McKinney finally saw the medical staff grow, as two more CME graduates were added. Dr. John Shaw had moved to Greeneville as a teenager. After completing medical school and serving a stint in the United States Navy, he returned to Takoma with his friend Dr. Michael Odell. They joined the medical staff in 1968. At age 80, Coolidge stopped practicing medicine and moved from Greeneville, leaving the hospital in the hands of a capable young staff.

Today, Takoma Regional houses 100 acute-care beds and extends the healing mission of Christ. It is likely that none of this would have happened had it not been for a surgeon's prayer many years ago and many miles away, in a place called Takoma Park.

SOURCES

Coolidge, L.E., "Founder Relates History of Takoma Hospital and Sanitarium," *The Greeneville Sun*, May 11, 1948, reprinted in Takoma Regional Hospital's 60th anniversary brochure, 1988.

Moore, Raymond S., *China Doctor: The Life Story of Harry Willis Miller*. Mt. View, California: Pacific Press Publishing Association, 1969.

Interview: Dr. James Ray McKinney.

Forty-five Cent Refund

Porter Adventist Hospital: Denver, Colorado | Founded 1930

Denver businessman Henry Porter sometimes spent the winter with his daughter in Southern California. On one of these visits in 1903, he came down with a cold, and she suggested that he go to Glendale Sanitarium for a hydrotherapy treatment. He found it so relaxing that he fell asleep on the treatment table. When he tried to give his therapist a one-dollar tip, the young man replied that the sanitarium paid him and it wouldn't be right to accept a tip, too. Porter would not forget that young employee's integrity.

About 25 years later, while staying near San Diego, Porter again came down with a bad cold. He asked whether there was an Adventist health center in the area and was referred to Paradise Valley Sanitarium in National City. Again he was impressed with the spirit of service the staff provided. He especially admired the kindness of a student nurse caring for an old man with Parkinson's disease.

Bookkeeping at Paradise Valley was done by hand in 1928, and the patients' journal was balanced at the end of each week. One week the clerk found a 45-cent overcharge in Porter's account. Credit manager Harley Rice immediately mailed a refund check with an apology. Porter promptly returned the check, claiming it was he who was indebted to the sanitarium staff:

> *Dear Sir: Your letter of 10th with [a] check for 45 cents [was] received, and I thank you for it and return it to you for credit [to] your general fund. I feel I have underpaid you all for your kind and careful treatment and attention, and I owe you all a debt of gratitude for the kind consideration while with you. Mrs. Porter and I are well, and I am gaining strength daily. With our regards and best wishes to you all.*

A couple of months later, Porter inquired about the possibility of building a facility in Denver similar to the ones in California. He was directed to church officials, and as a result, he and his daughter, Dora Porter Mason, gave $330,000 to build the Porter Sanitarium and Hospital on 40 acres that had been part of the original Porter family estate. At that time it represented the largest single gift ever received by the Adventist church. An additional $50,000 gift was used to build a nurses' dormitory called Dora Porter Mason Hall, which today houses some of the hospital offices.

Porter's interest in the hospital was clearly evident in his detailed suggestions to church leaders. He made a pencil sketch of the design he envisioned, which included landscaping, a dormitory, an artesian well, an 11-acre pasture, and a 20-acre field to be planted with corn and alfalfa. He even specified that a fence be built of "Colorado Special Wire."

Ground was broken in February 1929, with the earth so frozen that a fire had to be built to thaw it enough for the shovels to break through. One year later, on February 16, 1930, between 4,000 and 5,000 guests attended the grand opening of the 80-bed hospital. Unfortunately, Mr. Porter was sick with the flu and unable to attend.

Starting a hospital at the beginning of the Great Depression brought many challenges, and the Porter's early years were understandably difficult. Many patients could not pay their bills and sometimes their physicians paid the bill for them, even though they were having their own financial difficulties. Employee salaries were reduced at least three times.

While the Adventists assured Porter that they would run the hospital debt-free, he was sympathetic to their financial difficulties during those early years. He had a room at the hospital where he occasionally stayed for hydrotherapy treatments. However, without regard for his generosity in establishing the hospital, he paid for these services as though he were a stranger.

Delos Reeder came to the Porter San at the end of 1941 and got a job as a callboy, receiving 27 cents an hour. He recalled:

> *We did a lot of work then that is not done by anybody now because at that time, oxygen was not piped to the patient rooms. We had the old 100-pound tanks that I used to take to the rooms. I'd get the portable oxygen tent out of storage, and then fill the canister with ice. After I got everything plugged in and running, a nurse came in and set the amount of oxygen.*

When they weren't doing anything else, the callboys stood at the front door to welcome guests and visitors. This "welcome" meant helping sanitarium patients with their trunks and suitcases that contained all their personal items needed for a lengthy stay.

"We had to move all their stuff into the rooms—private rooms with rugs on the floor," Reeder recalled. "We were more or less bellhops to them when they needed help. They just lived there for months."

Reeder also remembered the severe shortage of employee housing that beset Porter during World War II. Some workers lived in the hospital, and several single women lived in the nurses' dormitory. This situation changed after the war when "The Courts" apartments were built from recycled military barracks, which Reeder helped move from the Fort Carson U.S. Army base in Colorado Springs. For nearly 30 years The Courts housed employees and interns as well as offices.

> "Our great burden is not that this new institution shall be a great, outstanding financial success, but rather that it shall find its place in the purpose of God and become the blessing in its community that its altruistic donors have purposed."
>
> — CHARLES RICE, BUSINESS MANAGER

One of the Porter's notable leaders was Harley Rice, the son of the hospital's second business manager, Charlie Rice, and the young man who sent Henry Porter the 45-cent refund in 1928.

When his office telephone rang, Harley Rice always answered, "Rice speaking." Perhaps not even he realized how much of a habit this had become until one Sabbath morning during church service when he offered prayer. Dr. John Davis recalled how members of the congregation knelt, bowed their heads, and closed their eyes. In the silence of the moment, the hospital business manager began to pray:

"Rice speaking," he said.

While those attending church that morning may not remember the rest of his prayer, no one was in doubt as to who offered it, not even the Lord.

Long-time employees, physicians, and volunteers agree that the people at Porter Sanitarium and Hospital were like a big family. They remember enjoying picnics and ballgames on the front lawn, packing fruit baskets for employees at Christmas, making fruitcakes for special friends of the hospital, and helping each other during snowstorms.

Two members of the Porter hospital family—sisters Lila Fehrer and Irene Howe—joined the hospital in 1958. Fehrer was secretary to the administrator for 25 years, and Howe retired with 30 years of service. Howe started as a medical transcriptionist. Her medical terminology at the time was limited to "appendectomy" and "tonsillectomy." With the help of a medical dictionary and the kindness of her co-workers, her vocabulary quickly increased.

"I'd just say, 'I don't understand this at all,' and one of the others would come over and help me."

In addition, she observed a couple of autopsies.

"I thought, 'Oh, I don't know how I can handle this,'" she said. "I just had to disassociate myself and think of it as a learning experience."

Post World War II brought some unusual challenges to the Porter medical staff, which was not open to adding many new physicians. As a consequence, a group of doctors converted a tuberculosis sanatorium into a general hospital that became Swedish Medical Center, and a cooperative of sorts between the two facilities developed.

Over time the Porter hospital grew, expanding the physical facility and increasing the number of patient beds. When Porter's son, William E. Porter, died in 1959, he bequeathed to the hospital a residual portion of his estate, which amounted to one million dollars. This helped fund a $2.5 million addition. Subsequent building programs eventually brought the total patient beds to 369. With the medical staff pretty well developed, the arrival of Ron Sackett as administrator in 1978 brought a new focus on services and programs, and the relationship with Swedish eventually dissolved.

Today's Porter Adventist Hospital is known for its cardiovascular services, transplant program, state-of-the-art cancer center, and women's center for minimally invasive surgery. Additionally, Porter's success made it possible to build a sister hospital in Littleton and to support construction of Avista Adventist Hospital in Louisville, which replaced Boulder Memorial Hospital after it was sold in 1989.

Littleton Adventist Hospital came about when Porter officials learned that a California developer had purchased property south of Denver. They bought about 40 acres in the area and opened an 85-bed facility in 1989. It has grown to 201 beds and recently completed a $40 million expansion to meet the needs of a rapidly growing market.

While the Adventist hospitals in Colorado today stand as memorials to a Denver businessman with a generous heart, they also bear testimony to an unidentified therapist who turned down a one-dollar tip, a student nurse who compassionately cared for her elderly patient, a conscientious bookkeeper who returned a 45-cent overpayment, and countless others whose Christian service exemplifies the healing ministry of Christ.

SOURCES

Rymes, Marion, *Porter Memorial Hospital, Its Birth and Life*, Denver, Colorado: Porter Memorial Hospital, 1978.

Robinson, Dores Eugene, *The Story of Our Health Message*, Nashville, Tennessee: Southern Publishing Association. 1943.

"Sixty Years of Caring," Denver, Colorado: Porter Memorial Hospital, 1990.

Interviews: Dr. John Davis, Lila Fehrer, Irene Howe, Delos Reeder and Ron Sackett.

Resort Reborn

Florida Hospital Heartland Medical Center: Sebring, Florida | Founded 1948

Originally known as Walker Memorial Sanitarium and Hospital, today's Florida Hospital Heartland Medical Center traces its roots to an abandoned facility, which at various times housed a resort, health center, hotel, casino, and military training center. Adventists converted it into a hospital in 1948.

In 1925, a large hotel was built on the shores of Lake Lillian (known then as Highlands Lake). The resort attracted many vacationers seeking Florida's warm winter weather. In fact, business was so good that the owners added a casino and an 18-hole golf course. After the stock market crash of 1929, however, business declined and the place went bankrupt. The huge hotel and casino remained vacant until a woman named Helen Randle purchased it in 1936.

Claiming to be a doctor, Randle convinced Avon Park residents to invest in what she promised would be an innovative health-and-fitness center. After raising money for the project, she left town, presumably to recruit a staff, but was eventually arrested in Massachusetts for fraud. Then came World War II, and the U.S. Air Force used the Avon Park facility as a training center for aviation cadets—often referring to it as the "Country Club of the Air."

Baldwin scoured the countryside locating equipment and furnishings, much of it from military surplus sources. He could not believe his eyes as he stood before the open warehouse door of one of the surplus sites. The warehouse was full of equipment and furnishings from a World War II hospital ship—everything from beds and operating tables to sterilizers, chairs, and mattresses. "It's all yours," the government official said.

An Adventist minister from nearby Wauchula visited an Avon Park attorney named Pardee around 1947 to solicit a contribution to the church's annual Ingathering appeal for humanitarian activities. No doubt the minister mentioned the denomination's medical work. Pardee knew a little about Adventist hospitals because some of his family had been at the Washington Sanitarium in Maryland. He told the minister he would like to see a similar facility established in Avon Park.

Wasting no time, the minister informed church officials in Florida of the lawyer's interest, and they turned the matter over to A.C. Larson, administrator of the Florida Sanitarium in Orlando. Larson asked Marvyn and Marie Baldwin to visit Avon Park and determine the level of interest in the community at large. The Baldwins discovered that while the town's residents knew little about Seventh-day Adventists, they were very much interested in a hospital for Avon Park.

By this time, of course, the Air Force had moved out, leaving the property in the hands of the War Assets Administration. This meant a not-for-profit organization could buy it for a highly discounted price. The Adventists got it all—hotel, casino, and two aircraft hangers—at a 100 percent discount.

It would take $400,000 to convert the facility into a hospital, but local businessman Charlie Walker readily agreed to lead a campaign to raise $150,000 from the community. The Adventist church promised the balance.

Larson put Baldwin in charge of getting the hospital ready for business. With only three months to get the job done, he scoured the countryside locating equipment and furnishings, much of it from military surplus sources. When Baldwin was shown one of the surplus sites, he could not believe his eyes as he stood before the open warehouse door. It was full of equipment and furnishings from a World War II hospital ship—everything from beds and operating tables to sterilizers, chairs, and mattresses.

"It's all yours," the government official said. "You've got two days to get it out of here."

Baldwin immediately hired a truck and crew and started hauling loads to Avon Park. They emptied the warehouse within the two-day limit, and a few weeks later opened the doors of the 63-bed hospital.

The transformation of the abandoned military center into a hospital fell primarily into the hands of four "pioneer" families from the Florida San. Joining the Baldwins were Forrest and Odessa Boyd, John and Kitty Schmidt, and Harold and Wanda Brown—eight adults and six children in all. They may have been accountants, nurses, chefs, secretaries, and administrators by profession, but for three months they were painters, carpenters, scrubbers, and window washers.

They prepared their meals in a makeshift kitchen set up in the basement and ate together family style. The women shopped for groceries, and Schmidt, the hospital's first chef, prepared the meals.

"We paid only 50 cents a piece," remembered Marie Baldwin. "We had wonderful meals—and wonderful times. I can still see some of the children getting sleepy and lying under the dinner table."

Unfortunately, Charlie Walker died of a heart attack shortly before the community reached its campaign goal. To honor his leadership and the work he had devoted to the project, the board named the hospital Walker Memorial Sanitarium and Hospital. The "Sanitarium" part of the name was later dropped, but the name "Walker" remained for almost 50 years.

Initially, Adventists planned to offer a sanitarium-type program at Avon Park, and did so for a few years, attracting a small clientele who paid nine dollars a day for a room, meals, and one hydrotherapy treatment. But despite these efforts to establish a facility modeled after Battle Creek and other early Adventist centers, the post-World War II era brought dramatic changes to the world of health care. Extended stays in a resort-style environment gave way to acute-care general hospitals, thanks in part to advances in medicine and science.

"We went through the transition from non-paperwork and non-insurance to the age of insurance and government regulations," said Mrs. Baldwin.

She and her husband not only spearheaded the hospital project in Avon Park, they also started a church in the old casino. The organizational relationship between the hospital and the church was virtually indistinguishable. In fact, the church also shared the Walker name—Walker Memorial Hospital Church—even though the man for whom the hospital was named was not a Seventh-day Adventist.

The hospital grew over the years to serve the expanding community, adding satellite facilities in two nearby communities. A Lake Placid campus opened in 1982, and the hospital in Wauchula joined the Walker family in 1992. Eventually, the aging facility in Avon Park needed replacing, and a new, 101-bed facility called Florida Hospital Heartland Medical Center in nearby Sebring opened in 1997.

SOURCE

Interviews: Marvyn and Marie Baldwin, 1999.

Pearl in Paradise

Feather River Hospital: Paradise, California | Founded 1950

Dr. Merritt Horning envisioned an Adventist health care center in Paradise similar to the famous Battle Creek Sanitarium. It would offer a strong health education program as well as medical and surgical services delivered with lots of tender loving care. He shared this dream with his colleague Dr. Dean Hoiland in 1946, and soon they involved others in the project, including Drs. C.C. Landis and Glenn Blackwelder.

131

These men, along with some community leaders, obtained 35 acres of land from the Paradise Irrigation District for the price of back taxes, $3,500. They later purchased an additional 40 acres for $600. The founders bought the land in their own names and later deeded it to the corporation that would build Feather River Sanitarium and Hospital. It was a beautiful site overlooking the Feather River Canyon—rural, quiet, and away from traffic, everything Horning thought it should be.

Knowing of Dr. Edward Sutherland's work in Madison, Tennessee, Horning invited him to Paradise to see the site. Sutherland both surprised and disappointed the doctor because he did not immediately declare it a perfect place for a health care facility.

"What's wrong with it?" asked Horning.

"You'll need more land," Sutherland said. "Buy more land than you can ever imagine you'll want."

"How in the world will we ever get the money to buy more land when we haven't paid for what we already have?" Horning responded.

"How did the man in the Bible buy the pearl of great price?" Sutherland asked, reminding Horning of the familiar parable.

"He sold all he had and bought it."

"This is how you will purchase more land," Sutherland said.

It would take personal sacrifice, commitment from the community, and many answered prayers to bring Feather River Hospital into being, but the people in Paradise heeded the good counsel of Sutherland and eventually obtained a total of 107 acres. They were ready to begin construction in April 1948 despite the fact that they had not yet raised all of the needed funds. Rather than delay construction, they decided to omit the surgical and obstetrical units. With no collateral against which to borrow, 5 individuals signed notes guaranteeing the principal plus interest. Joining Landis, Horning, and Blackwelder were P.V. Harrigan, the county's agricultural commissioner, and Roy Rankin, a retired pharmacist.

Construction progressed slowly as funds came through the generosity of many hardworking people. Rankin opened a pharmacy for the express purpose of benefiting the hospital. Working for only $2.60 an hour, he generated $60,000 for the project. Landis and his wife sold some property for $5,000 and gave the proceeds to the hospital. S.L. Dombrosky from Oakland helped with public relations and fundraising. Many others helped in whatever ways they could.

Fernando Stahl, a retired missionary from South America, joined the Paradise effort as chaplain. He often called prayer groups together asking the Lord to bless the building program. The following experiences illustrate some of their answered prayers.

Horning decided to make a house call one morning in 1949 to visit one of his patients, Frank Digital. Seeing the doctor approaching his house, Digital met him at the door.

"Dr. Horning, what in the world are you doing here? Come in. I want to talk to you," he said, seeming excited and surprised by the doctor's visit.

Digital and his wife had just finished praying, asking God to provide a use for some money they had available for a special project. The doctor's arrival seemed to be an answer to their prayer, and Digital wrote him a check for $2,500.

In another instance of divine provision, a local woman told Horning, "My husband is a hard-headed old Swede. He will not loan money or give money to anybody for anything."

She explained that she had prayed, asking God to impress upon her husband the needs of the hospital—even suggesting that she would be willing to undergo surgery if that would soften his heart.

At the time of this prayer, she had no indication that she needed surgery. But within weeks, doctors found an abdominal tumor, and she had to be transported out of town for the procedure. A few weeks later she returned to the doctor's office for a checkup—accompanied by her husband with a $10,000 check. He later doubled his gift.

Victor and Edith Hoag, patients of Blackwelder, entered his office one day carrying a round container similar to a large mailing tube. Mr. Hoag ceremoniously began pulling bills from it and placing them on the doctor's desk. As the stacks of bills grew taller and taller, it seemed to Blackwelder that the little green papers would never stop coming. When the last bill had been drawn from the tube, their gift totaled $2,500.

God answered prayers in many ways, not only through the provision of financial resources. For instance, a heavy rainstorm hit Paradise at the same time the lumber for construction was being delivered from Reno, Nevada. Another prayer meeting was held, and miraculously, the rain seemed to fall everywhere except on the lumber shipment.

The hospital project convinced many people in Paradise that no problem is too big for God. In applying for a license, the doctors learned that the facility had to include a surgical unit. This seemed like an impossible roadblock—until Horning called the state director of public health. This gentleman, Dr. Wilton Halvarsen, had been one of Horning's teachers in medical school. When Horning explained the situation, Halvarsen told him not to worry. Within days, the state had created a new hospital classification to accommodate the Paradise project, and Feather River Sanitarium and Hospital received a license as an acute medical facility with 18 beds.

The hospital opened on December 7, 1950. Patients in private rooms paid 16 dollars a day, and those in ward beds paid 12 dollars. All patients received physical therapy and hydrotherapy as standard services at no additional charge.

In the beginning, employees made personal sacrifices to help ensure the hospital's financial viability. For example, during the first three months, nurses worked for only half of their pay, and local merchants funded the payroll. Zula Ahl, the first superintendent of nurses, received only $250 a month. In addition, the founding physicians gave their professional fees to the hospital.

> In the beginning, employees made personal sacrifices to help ensure the hospital's financial viability...during the first three months, nurses worked for only half of their pay, and local merchants funded the payroll. ... the first superintendent of nurses received only $250 a month. In addition, the founding physicians gave their professional fees to the hospital.

Feather River was the "first and only" in many respects. For example, it was the only hospital in the region that trained nursing assistants. It also offered training for teen volunteers called candy stripers (girls) and handy stripers (boys).

The hospital itself grew many of the fruits and vegetables served to the patients and employees. Herbert White, grandson of Adventist pioneers James and Ellen G. White, developed a program designed to "remineralize" the soil and produce highly nutritional foods. This was a big selling point in the sanitarium's early marketing brochures.

Feather River Sanitarium and Hospital was the first public building in Butte County to prohibit smoking, much to the chagrin of the patients who could not smoke in their rooms and of local businessmen who accused the physicians of imposing their personal beliefs onto the public. The physicians, however, held fast to their position that smoking tobacco was a health hazard and a public pollutant. The "No Smoking" signs remained posted on the walls, and patients smoked in designated areas only. In time, of course, science supported the doctors' position, and public attitudes toward the hospital's policy changed from criticism to appreciation.

✳

Within the first year, it became clear that the hospital needed obstetrical and surgery services. One convincing incident occurred during a winter storm when an expectant mother went into labor. With the roads closed, her husband made an ambulance out of his wheelbarrow and pushed his wife through the snow all the way to the hospital. The staff had to improvise a delivery room, and having no bassinet, they placed the baby in a dresser drawer.

Other needs soon became apparent. Lack of a surgical suite meant patients had to be transferred out of town for operations. Feather River finally added its own surgery unit in 1952, but the building's construction made it necessary to transport patients outdoors. Always accompanied by an anesthesiologist and surgeon, patients were wheeled on gurneys around one end of the building to the surgery area. Bad weather may have occasionally delayed a surgery, but the staff kept patients appropriately protected from rain or snow.

"I don't want prayer," the patient insisted. The nurses, however, politely persisted and finally one night he gave in. "Okay, then. If you must, pray!" That experience was a turning point, and from then on he wanted a nurse to pray with him every night.

Feather River Hospital was successful from the day it opened because it offered physical therapy, hydrotherapy, and health education at a level not then offered by other medical facilities in the area. About 70 percent of patients in the early years came from out of town. One of these was California's 55-year-old assistant treasurer from Sacramento. He suffered from lung cancer and had only about three months to live.

"I've been to all the specialists in Sacramento, and they can't offer me anything. What can you do for me?" he asked.

Horning said they would give him an abundance of tender loving care and make him comfortable with hydrotherapy and whatever medications were indicated.

"I'll take it," the man said.

He moved to the sanitarium, where he enjoyed the extraordinary nursing care and the physical therapy and hydrotherapy treatments. But he wanted no part of the prayers the nurses offered each evening.

"I don't want prayer," he insisted.

The nurses, however, politely persisted and finally one night he gave in.

"Okay, then. If you must, pray!"

That experience was a turning point, and from then on he wanted a nurse to pray with him every night. Because he was a state official, he received many phone calls and visitors, which began to wear on him. About two weeks before he died, he posted the following message on his door to discourage such interruptions: "I want to spend the last days of my life with my family, and my family is the staff of the Feather River Hospital."

Two events prompted hospital leaders to take steps to ensure the facility's long-term mission as an Adventist health care center. Blackwelder died suddenly in 1954, and Landis died in 1958. Although consideration was briefly given to making Feather River a government rehabilitation center or a tax-supported community hospital, the owners decided to entrust it to the Seventh-day Adventist Church to be operated according to the founders' ideals and objectives. Church officials assumed their elected positions on the board of directors in 1960, and Feather River has continued in its original mission to treat the whole person and offer compassionate care.

SOURCE

Nye, Michelle, "The History of Feather River Hospital," 1999.

Golden Days in Sierra Foothills

Sonora Community Hospital: Sonora, California | Founded 1957

Dr. Ben Boice moved to the quiet town of Sonora in central California's Sierra Nevada foothills in 1950. Had he arrived 100 years earlier, he would have found a bustling gold rush town, populated by fortune-seeking miners and merchants from near and far. While most of the original miners came from Sonora, Mexico, hence the town's name, the lure of gold drew migrants from around the world.

Interestingly, it was the need for health care that brought the townspeople together for the first time as a community. Following an outbreak of scurvy in the winter of 1848-49, the townspeople set up a hospital, which operated during at least one rainy season.

Things had settled down considerably by the time Boice moved to Sonoma 100 years later to practice medicine. Although fewer than 4,000 people lived in the area, the community had three hospitals: Sonora Hospital, Columbia Way Hospital, and Tuolumne General Hospital. Receiving a less-than-friendly welcome in the local medical community, Boice bought Sonora Hospital in 1951. Dr. R. Innis Bromley had built the facility on the main street of town in 1908 at a cost of $1,500. First known as the Bromley Sanitarium, it was later renamed Sonora Hospital.

Drs. Helen and Paul Anspach joined Boice in 1954, and these three Loma Linda-trained physicians operated the small hospital for three or four years. Other Loma Linda graduates were also attracted to the area, including Dr. Ted Howard, who came in 1956 and remained on the medical staff until he retired in 1992.

"We were just starting our family. We were looking for a place that was out of the way, but not too far out of the way—a place that was beautiful, and above all else, had mountains and trees. Sonora was perfect for us," says Howard.

"We used a gurney when we had to take a patient upstairs. Four people would take hold of it. They would start upstairs, and when they came to the landings, they suspended the gurney over the open stairwell. We never dropped anybody, but I think we were just lucky."

– DR. TED HOWARD

He remembers the old hospital well. It was a two-story building with a full basement. Doctors' offices occupied the first floor, with a kitchen, laboratory, and physical therapy area in the basement, and the X-ray department and patient rooms on the second floor. All rooms had high ceilings, which helped keep them cool in summer. The biggest inconvenience was the lack of an elevator. A large central staircase with two landings provided the only access between floors. Dr. Howard recalled:

> *We used a gurney when we had to take a patient upstairs. Four people would take hold of it. They would start upstairs, and when they came to the landings, they suspended the gurney over the open stairwell. We never dropped anybody, but I think we were just lucky.*

Obviously, the historic building provided only a temporary home for the hospital. The Boices and Anspachs decided to build their own facility, and they purchased land on the outskirts of town. With the aid of federal funding, they built a 42-bed hospital in 1957.

Their aim was to build the finest hospital in the area. The one-story facility was the first to offer only private and two-bed patient rooms, each equipped with oxygen. The facility also boasted tiled surgery suites and delivery rooms, air-conditioning, and radiant heat. Patient rooms even had outlets for radio and television. Dr. Helen was the first administrator, a position she held for seven years.

After the hospital was built, more physicians moved to the area, but attracting other personnel remained a challenge. While Sonora was in a beautiful and interesting location, single nurses often found it to be a little more out of the way than they preferred, and married nurses needed assurance that their spouses would find jobs, too.

Boice and the Anspachs owned Sonora Community Hospital approximately four years, before donating it to the Central California Conference of Seventh-day Adventists. Although they were no longer the owners, they continued to manage it. Boice headed the hospital for the next eighteen years, from 1964 until 1981.

As was the case at many other Adventist hospital locations, a church and school were established on the same campus. Today's Seventh-day Adventist Church and 10-grade school are in large part the result of the influence of Sonora Community Hospital.

Over the years the hospital grew with the community. In addition to physical growth, time brought many changes, including a merger with another hospital in town in 1981. The hospital was renamed Sonora Regional Medical Center in 2004 and relocated to a $38 million, 152-bed facility where it continues to share God's love through physical, mental, and spiritual healing.

SOURCES

Benton, Pat Horning, "Sonora Community Hospital continues to offer Christian services to the Central California Sierra foothills," *Pacific Union Recorder*, October 6. 1997.

The City of Sonora website.

Interviews: Eloice Boice, Doris Fletcher Mills (local historian) and Ted Howard.

Battle Creek Revisited

Battle Creek Health Center: Battle Creek, Michigan | 1957–1993

The Battle Creek Sanitarium under Kellogg's leadership remained on the list of Seventh-day Adventist institutions until 1906. Although Kellogg controlled the facility until he died in 1943, his relationship with the Seventh-day Adventist Church was always controversial. The world-famous San acquired enormous debt in the late 1920s, and with the depression of the 1930s, it went into receivership. The government bought the main building in 1942, which helped pay off some of the debt.

Hospital Board President George MacKay had promised Kellogg that he would keep the facility open, but by 1957 this no longer appeared feasible. Members of the medical staff had either died or planned to retire soon. MacKay had little choice but to liquidate the assets.

When Allen Vandeman from the Hinsdale Sanitarium near Chicago heard of MacKay's plans, he drove to Battle Creek to see if something could be done to return the sanitarium to the church. After meeting with MacKay, he notified a group of physicians in Glendale, California to gauge their interest in operating it. Among them were Drs. Dunbar Smith and J. Wayne McFarland.

At age 11, Lady Bird Johnson had visited the Battle Creek Sanitarium with an aunt. She spoke at the facility's centennial celebration, recalling her memories of Dr. John Harvey Kellogg riding his bicycle to work. At the San, she said, she had learned "the importance of vitamins, sunshine, and exercise."

"Wouldn't it be wonderful if we could recover the old Battle Creek Sanitarium, mother of all Adventist medical institutions?" thought Smith.

The doctors flew to Battle Creek to investigate the idea and returned with a positive impression. But before committing to the project, Smith sought counsel from George Nelson, administrator of the Glendale Sanitarium, and officials at the denomination's Lake Union Conference and Michigan Conference. Each visit buoyed his desire to proceed with the acquisition.

It would take $300,000 to get the Battle Creek Sanitarium out of receivership—an amount the doctors were in no position to pay. Two of them had recently returned from the mission field, one had just completed a residency and another was still in residency. They would need to look elsewhere for funding.

According to Smith, the team was advised to seek funding from a holding corporation that had been set up to receive payments from the settlement between the church and the sanitarium. The church had earmarked the funds for medical work in Michigan.

They followed this advice, and the church agreed to give the physicians $200,000 from the fund on the condition that they raise the remaining $100,000. Not knowing where they would get that kind of money, the doctors made it a matter of prayer, relying on the Lord to supply their need. And indeed He did.

Arrangements were made for them to meet with Dr. Charles E. Stewart, Jr., son of Dr. Kellogg's right hand man at Battle Creek.

"'I'll loan you $50,000 without interest. Will that help?'" Stewart offered.

The doctors assured him it would.

Stewart left the room so the doctors could discuss the matter, but returned a short time later and offered them another $30,000. While this donation left the doctors short of their goal by only $20,000, they may as well have needed a million dollars. They simply didn't have it. One last time Stewart left the room and returned to their meeting, this time offering to mortgage his office for $20,000. And with that generous gesture, the doctors at last had all they needed to acquire the Battle Creek San.

Smith and McFarland next traveled to Battle Creek to prepare for the court hearing and acquisition of the property. Their colleagues in Glendale were scheduled to join them later. Although the paperwork appeared to be complete and in order the day before the hearing, the $200,000 payment had not yet arrived from the holding corporation. Smith called the Lake Union Conference office only to learn that the president was traveling to Washington, D.C., and the treasurer was on vacation. He finally reached the union president by telephone, but little could be done from Washington.

"Time is too short, and I have no checks with me," the president said.

"Please, do what you can. Everything depends on having the full amount when we meet with the judge tomorrow," begged Smith.

A short time later, the doctor received a call from the president of the Michigan Conference in Lansing. He planned to attend a school board meeting in Battle Creek and would bring the $200,000 check with him that evening. Smith and McFarland waited and waited, but the man never showed up. When it came time to go to bed, they still did not have the money, and their colleagues were arriving from Los Angeles the next morning. Again Smith and McFarland prayed for God to meet their need.

No sooner had they fallen asleep than the phone rang. The call was from the doctors in Glendale. They were ready to board a red-eye flight to Michigan and wanted to make sure everything was ready for the hearing. Without mentioning the $200,000 problem, Smith told them to come. The Lord had faithfully answered his prayers in the past, and he believed the money would be in his hands before the deadline. However, when he met his Glendale friends at the airport the next morning, he still did not have the check.

The group gathered for the hearing with only Smith and McFarland aware of the problem. While they were waiting, Dr. Leland McElmurry, a physician from Lansing, arrived. McElmurry had been invited to join the sanitarium's new board of directors, and the conference office sent him to the hearing—with the check. A telegram was sent to church headquarters in Washington, D.C., announcing that the Battle Creek Sanitarium was back in the hands of the church.

When the Battle Creek Sanitarium had first opened in 1866, Andrew Johnson was president of the United States. One hundred years later another President Johnson signed the guest registry at the resurrected sanitarium's centennial celebration—Lyndon Johnson, accompanied by his wife Lady Bird.

At age 11, Mrs. Johnson had visited the sanitarium with an aunt. She spoke at the centennial celebration of her memories of Dr. John Harvey Kellogg riding his bicycle to work. At the San, she said, she had learned "the importance of vitamins, sunshine, and exercise." As a memento of her visit, the administrator presented her with her original sanitarium admission card.

The Battle Creek Sanitarium, renamed Battle Creek Health Center, operated for several years as a self-supporting organization. A mental health unit and alcohol and drug rehabilitation programs helped to strengthen its financial base. The Adventist church took over the hospital in 1974 and operated it until financial difficulties led to its closure in 1993.

SOURCES

Robinson, D.E., *The Story of Our Health Message*, Nashville, Tennessee: Southern Publishing Association. 1965.

Smith, Dunbar W., M.D., *The Travels, Triumphs and Vicissitudes of Dunbar W. Smith, M.D.*, Loma Linda, California: Dunbar W. Smith, M.D., 1994.

Homegrown in America's Heartland

Shawnee Mission Medical Center: Shawnee Mission, Kansas | Founded 1962

Months of searching for an affordable site for a new hospital in suburban Kansas City had proven fruitless. Finally, multi-millionaire developer, Miller Nichols, invited a group of Adventists to look at a prime piece of property that would eventually border Interstate 35. Indeed, it was a perfect location for a hospital, but the Adventists had no money to buy such a valuable piece of real estate. Nichols, however, had no intention of selling it to them. He donated it—a gift appraised at well over $650,000 in the 1960s.

Shawnee and Mission were two of many small farm towns that became linked by suburban communities that grew up around Kansas City after World War II. For convenience, the U.S. Postal Service designated the entire area as "Shawnee Mission."

Today it is difficult to imagine this populous corner of Johnson County without a modern health care facility, but in the mid-1950s, this was all farmland. Certain business and community leaders, however, saw a population boom coming. Among other things, they recognized the need for a hospital in the communities that were growing up around Kansas City—an idea strongly opposed by the large downtown hospitals.

Yet some physicians did not share this mentality and actually preferred to practice in the suburbs. Dr. Donald Smith and other members of the Johnson County Medical Society succeeded in persuading the state legislature to approve a bill in 1955 that allowed the county townships to proceed with financing and planning of a hospital. However, the county's voters—already financially stretched to build roads, sewers, and other infrastructure—flatly rejected a mill levy that would have funded the project.

A year or so later, members of the recently established New Haven Seventh-day Adventist Church in nearby Overland Park began considering the launch of a medical missionary project. They had in mind a self-supporting organization modeled somewhat after Madison College and Madison Sanitarium and Hospital in Tennessee. To that end, they chartered a not-for-profit corporation and began making plans to build.

Hearing of the Adventists' plans, local community leaders urged them to build a full-service hospital. With no public money available, Paul Jackson, a minister on medical leave at that time, raised funds in the community. In faith, the small group of church members began building a hospital and health center.

After the medical society enthusiastically endorsed plans for the new facility, the community undertook a major fundraising campaign. Ground was broken early in 1961, and later that same year the health center opened with 100 long-term care beds. Though lacking sufficient income to pay current bills, hospital leaders again moved ahead in faith and opened a 65-bed acute-care hospital in 1962.

The hospital faced almost insurmountable financial difficulties in its early years. Stories are told of board meetings lasting all night, as the directors tried to resolve the problems. Some even mortgaged their homes to raise money for the hospital. Finally, Shawnee Mission Medical Center was transferred to the Central Union Conference of Seventh-day Adventists. Russell Shawver from Kettering Memorial Hospital in Ohio was appointed administrator.

> The hospital faced almost insurmountable financial difficulties in its early years. Stories are told of board meetings lasting all night, as the directors tried to resolve the problems. Some even mortgaged their homes to raise money for the hospital.

The new administrator was in the middle of moving and was scheduled to go on vacation before taking over his new position when news calling for immediate action hit the front page of the *Kansas City Star*. A proprietary hospital corporation had announced plans to build a 400-bed facility in the exploding Shawnee Mission suburbs, only about five miles from the Shawnee Mission Medical Center. Competition from a large, well-funded, for-profit facility was the last thing the struggling 200-bed hospital needed.

Shawver called an architectural firm he had worked with previously and explained the situation. When he returned from vacation, plans for a new hospital were on his desk. The hospital board met to review them, and within days the local newspapers announced Shawnee Mission's plan to expand to 400 beds.

Before either hospital could begin construction, each had to go through the certificate-of-need (CON) process, a relatively new and laborious requirement. Both hospitals filed at the same time, and each was eventually approved.

In the meantime, detailed plans were being drawn for the new Shawnee Mission hospital. Knowing that steel was in short supply and orders could be delayed for several weeks or months, Shawver purchased all the steel needed to build the new hospital and stored it.

"If this falls through, we'll have enough steel to build a ship to sail to South America—and we'll probably have to!" he told his wife.

Throughout the CON process, Shawver worked to develop important support for the expansion among the medical staff, as well as the community. This proved invaluable when it came to obtaining an endorsement for the municipal bonds to fund the construction project.

The new hospital attracted physicians and patients even before it was completed. In fact, part of the new construction had to be built above and around a section of the existing structure. This allowed for the care of patients throughout construction. After a new section was completed, patient beds were moved out, and the old structure—enclosed by the new—was demolished. The new 383-bed Shawnee Mission Medical Center opened in 1977, with then U.S. Senator Bob Dole present for the dedication.

Recent years have brought the hospital continued growth and public recognition.

The original hospital campus of 4.3 acres has grown to 54 acres that house a freestanding outpatient surgery facility, a health education building, five medical office buildings, an employee child care center, and a community fitness course.

SOURCES

"There Was a Dream," undated hospital document.

Interviews: Russell Shawver and Bob Woolford.

Hawaiians Wait for Hospital

Castle Medical Center: Kailua, Hawaii | Founded 1963

Adventist missionaries arrived in the Hawaiian Islands in the late 1800s. Sometime in the late 1890s, Dr. Preston Kellogg, brother of Dr. John Harvey Kellogg, started a sanitarium in downtown Honolulu, which operated for only a short while. Sixty years later and after many changes in the world of health care, a local community invited the church to help establish a permanent hospital in Hawaii.

In 1950, Dr. Robert Chung returned to his home state of Hawaii after graduating from medical school in Loma Linda, California. At that time, residents of Windward Oahu had only part-time ambulance service over the old Pali Road. This steep mountain road was prone to rockslides during the island's frequent rains.

Chung was a well-known physician in the community and part of a small group that launched a campaign in 1959 to establish an Adventist hospital in Windward Oahu. Carolyn Rankin, another community leader, was also a strong proponent of the hospital, and ranch owner Harold Castle donated 10 acres of property for the building site.

The community raised $170,000, and the Seventh-day Adventist Church offered $600,000 towards construction. In addition, both the Governor's Hospital Advisory Council and the 30th Territorial Legislature backed the project. But even with these commitments, a hospital for Windward Oahu remained at a standstill because the board of health refused to designate the chosen property as a separate hospital zone, thus delaying federal funds for construction.

> Known for its outstanding community health and wellness programs, as well as its mission of "Caring for our community... Sharing God's love," Castle Medical Center is the primary health-care facility for Windward Oahu.

According to long-time hospital board member Luther Park, the powers that be at that time did not want to create competition for the existing Honolulu hospitals. A series of articles in *The Honolulu Advertiser* chronicled the community's seven-year struggle with the board of health. Unfortunately, the controversy was not settled until two tragic incidents pointed out the critical need for a hospital on Windward Oahu.

First, five men were injured when the roof collapsed at a nearly completed department store in Kailua. The next month, a two-year-old girl choked to death. Doctors in Honolulu said her life might have been saved had there been a hospital operating room close to her home in Kailua. The following month, the state board of health approved the proposed hospital.

The $2 million, 72-bed hospital opened on January 16, 1963. Known for a while as Windward Oahu Hospital, it was officially named Castle Memorial Hospital in honor of the man who donated the land on which it was built. Today Castle Medical Center is a 160-bed award-winning hospital serving all of Oahu. Known for its outstanding community health and wellness programs, as well as its mission of "Caring for our community…Sharing God's love," it is the primary health care facility for Windward Oahu.

SOURCES

Judd, Wayne, tape recorded interview with Erwin Remboldt, 1998.

Interview: Luther Park.

Built on Excellence

Kettering Medical Center: Kettering, Ohio | Founded 1964

When Charles F. Kettering died in 1958, his family decided to build a hospital in his memory on the family estate near Dayton, Ohio. It seemed only natural that the Ketterings would build a hospital to honor the famous engineer, scientist, inventor, philosopher, and philanthropist. Keenly interested in health care, he had co-founded the Sloan-Kettering Cancer Institute in New York, a global leader in cancer research and treatment. However, he was most recognized for his many inventions, including the first successful self-starter for the automobile, a dependable ignition system, four-wheel brakes, and the first quick-drying paint, which made it possible to paint cars on an assembly line.

In the early 1950s, Charles Kettering's son, Eugene, had discussed with his physician, Dr. Douglas Talbott, the idea of establishing a research institute and small hospital on the Kettering estate. With $5,000 from Kettering, Talbott proceeded with plans for a research center and 50-bed hospital. He employed an architectural firm and filed an application for Hill-Burton funds. Later, however, community leaders informed Kettering that a study revealed a need for a 300- to 400-bed facility in the southern part of the city. As a result, they were hesitant to support Talbott's effort.

Based on their experience in the 1940s and 1950s with the Hinsdale Sanitarium and Hospital in Illinois, the family decided the new facility should be an Adventist hospital. Eugene and Virginia Kettering and their children did not choose the Adventists because of their worldwide medical work or management skills, although these were important, said George Nelson, first president of the medical center. The Ketterings had been most impressed by the compassion and quality of patient care they had seen at Hinsdale Sanitarium and Hospital near Chicago. Living only a short distance from the sanitarium, they had personally assisted in the care of patients during a polio epidemic in 1949 and had spearheaded a major building campaign at Hinsdale. They also had met people such as Jessie Tupper.

"It was she, and those with whom she worked, who provided the superior patient care with a skillful yet 'tender touch' that so attracted the Ketterings. They looked up to her as an example of what they thought Adventist nurses should be. To them, she was a modern Florence Nightingale," Nelson wrote.

This quality was what the Ketterings wanted in a hospital to honor Charles F. Kettering. Some months after his death, family members met with representatives of the Adventists' Columbia Union Conference and General Conference. After securing appropriate committee approvals, the church agreed to the proposed hospital. Nelson, who had served 20 years at the Glendale Sanitarium and Hospital in California, accepted the responsibility of heading the Kettering program.

Eugene Kettering said that he had always intended for the hospital to be built and operated by the Adventist church. A few people in the Dayton community were already aware of the church's medical work. General Motors executives, for example, had sometimes used Adventist hospitals while on overseas assignments. Also, the founder of National Cash Register Company had been a patient of Dr. John Harvey Kellogg at Battle Creek. In fact, he had brought two Battle Creek therapists back to Dayton to set up a physical therapy treatment facility in his office building.

After seeing the facility, the group returned to Dayton, called a meeting, and after about 20 minutes pledged $1.5 million for a new hospital. Within six months, total gifts amounted to over $1.9 million.

Once Kettering had acquired the church's commitment to build the hospital, he arranged for a group of community leaders to visit the Hinsdale Sanitarium and Hospital. Mardian Blair, then assistant administrator, organized the hospital tour. After seeing the facility, the group returned to Dayton, called a meeting, and after about 20 minutes pledged $1.5 million for a new hospital. Within six months, total gifts amounted to over $1.9 million.

On his first visit to Dayton in November 1959, Nelson learned that Kettering had opened a million-dollar bank account in his name.

"What a demonstration of confidence!" Nelson thought. There was no organization yet, no written agreement, no building, no staff. The two men had not even met. The next few years, of course, proved that Kettering's confidence had been well placed.

Harley Rice, associate secretary of the General Conference Medical Department in Washington, D.C., joined Nelson on a subsequent visit. They planned to meet with physicians of the county medical society who had been working with the architects on the Talbott project. In preparation for the meeting, Nelson and Rice rented a typewriter and spent an afternoon rehearsing answers to questions they anticipated the physicians would ask. That evening they were met with an icy reception.

"Figuratively, we picked the icicles off the wall as we made our way around the room," Nelson said.

The chairman wasted no time in getting down to business. He announced that the physicians had prepared some questions for the visitors. Rice responded with a smile.

"In anticipation of this meeting we have prepared the answers," he said, placing the typewritten papers on the table. Slowly the ice began to melt.

One of the county medical society doctors had visited Hinsdale Hospital, and he recounted his conversations with some of the physicians there. They had told him that they preferred to practice at Hinsdale because of the equipment, cleanliness, and quality of patient care.

Nelson and Rice left the meeting believing it had been successful. The next day, however, brought new challenges to resolve, as several changes had to be made to the original plans if they were to create the major teaching facility that Nelson envisioned the Kettering hospital would be. For one, Nelson knew he must nurture the philosophy of excellence and compassion that had attracted the Ketterings to Adventist health care in the first place. This perspective had to be apparent as soon as a person walked into the door of the facility. He insisted that the interior decoration "create a warm, welcoming atmosphere with emphasis on comfort; privacy where indicated; beauty without ostentation; and, wherever possible, a touch of class."

He also insisted on an auditorium. When the architect said there was no money in the budget for an auditorium, Nelson paid a visit to the Ketterings' attorney. He explained he needed the auditorium to help "create and keep alive forever an atmosphere of gentle, caring, scientifically-sound Christian service for all who come seeking help…" To do that, he continued, "…we must have ready access to groups of employees with whom we [can] discuss effective ways of meeting these ultimate goals."

When this explanation reached Kettering, he said, "[It] is exactly what we want," and Nelson got the auditorium.

The changes Nelson and Rice made to the original plans would significantly delay construction. The earlier application for a $1 million Hill-Burton grant had been approved with the stipulation that construction would begin by July 1, 1960. Now there was no way to make all the changes and meet that deadline. A new application had to be filed, but instead of one million dollars, the revised project received nearly $2.5 million.

Nelson did not personally meet Kettering until March 1960, at which time he suggested preparing some documents detailing the agreement. Kettering's response has become a memorable part of the medical center's history:

"What's the matter, George, don't you trust me?" he asked.

Nelson said he soon learned "that Eugene Kettering's word needed no extra certification."

Virginia Kettering also played a key role in developing Kettering Medical Center, particularly in such details as the smiling animal faces on the walls in the pediatric unit and a gift shop featuring many items she personally selected on her travels.

Nelson set up an office in downtown Dayton and hired a small staff—a secretary, a plant engineer, a director of nursing service and education, and a chief financial officer. In addition to constructing the hospital and recruiting top-quality leaders, he spent a lot of time in the community keeping abreast of concerns and answering questions.

Finding 500 to 600 employees to staff the new hospital was an enormous undertaking. Nelson knew the Ketterings had been impressed with the people at Hinsdale and that he must bring in a team of professionals who epitomized excellence. Because he had promised not to recruit employees from other Dayton hospitals, he had to move people from other parts of the country, thus adding to the new hospital's expenses.

Nelson began organizing the medical staff in June 1960, calling together a number of individuals from the county medical society. Knowing they had questions about the Sabbath and Adventist diet, he addressed the matters directly:

> *…I explained the Seventh-day Adventist philosophy regarding patient care on the Sabbath; described the Sabbath as a day for healing; and that everything necessary for care, comfort, and safety of patients would be done, but that elective surgery would not be scheduled, and all routine work other than patient care would be done on other days…I described Adventist views on diet, indicating that such views were a matter of health, not of church doctrine.*

The day before Kettering Memorial Medical Center officially opened on February 16, 1964, Rice made one of the first presentations in the new auditorium. The following is an excerpt of that address to the employees:

> *This hospital is truly an administrator's dream. You have everything that money can buy. You have a stupendous task in the next few weeks of putting in place all the new equipment.*

You will be completely occupied and preoccupied in testing it and synchronizing it into a smoothly operating service. This equipment is needed to make a hospital; it is necessary. Insofar as financial resources can provide the necessary tools, this hospital is compelled to be a success.

But do you have an adequate stock of those things that money can't buy? I think of the words of Jesus to Martha when He visited her house: "Martha, my dear, you are careful about many things. But only a few things are needed, perhaps only one."

You have the many. But what are these few things? What is the one? I believe the few things that are needed are attitudes. Boards can vote policies, but attitudes determine whether or not they will work. Money can provide equipment, but attitudes determine its ultimate usefulness.

People will come here from many different backgrounds and walks of life. The blending process will tax your full measure of adaptability, the tensile strength of your understanding, and the capacity of your charity. Attitudes will make or break the team. No committee can write a job description of these attitudes. No board can vote them. Yet without them the building is but an empty shell.

"Only a few things are needed, perhaps one." What is that one? I believe that one thing that can't be bought is purpose—objective. Your objective here is to heal the body and the spirit. Those who come in direct contact with patients will contribute much. Those who work behind the scenes will be important, too.

Dayton expects much of you. Will you give that indefinable something—purpose, objective, reason for existence—which will produce even more than is expected? It is yours to give. Give to every new worker. Give without stint to every patient.

As his friendship and working relationship with the Ketterings grew, Nelson became more determined to create an institution that would meet their high standards.

Now known as Kettering Medical Center, the 508-bed facility serves the greater Dayton area as part of the regional acute-care Kettering Health Network. This seven-hospital system also includes Grandview Hospital, Southview Hospital, Sycamore Hospital, as well as other related organizations.

SOURCES

Nelson, George, *The Kettering Medical Center: Recollections and Reflections on the Early Years,* 1996.

Schaefer, Richard A., *Legacy: Daring to Care*, Loma Linda, California: Legacy Publishing Association, 1995.

Interview: George Nelson.

Every Dollar Counts

Manchester Memorial Hospital: Manchester, Kentucky | Founded 1971

Modern health care came to Clay County, Kentucky partly to end the famous family feuds that resulted in hundreds of horrible injuries and deaths between 1865 and 1915. One of the bloodiest of these clan wars reportedly occurred in Manchester. In an effort to stop the fighting, James Anderson Burns established a Baptist school in nearby Oneida. While traveling the countryside raising funds for the school, he met Dr. C. Adeline McConville, who hoped to build a hospital for mountain women.

Sometime in the late 1920s, the Oneida Mountain Hospital opened. The state operated it as a maternity hospital for about 10 years, staffing it with resident physicians from the University of Kentucky. The charge to deliver a baby was only one dollar, without regard to the patient's ability to pay. When funding ran out in 1952, the hospital closed. Having heard that Seventh-day Adventists ran hospitals, someone in the community called the church's headquarters in Washington, D.C. Eventually the church agreed to operate the Oneida Mountain Hospital through its Kentucky-Tennessee Conference.

Herb Atherton was the hospital administrator for seven years. Robert Pierson, then president of the Kentucky-Tennessee Conference, also invited Dr. Caleb Chu, an Adventist physician originally from China, to practice in Oneida. Chu had worked as a houseboy for Madame Chiang Kai-shek, who paid his way through nursing school at the Shanghai Sanitarium. While there he became a Seventh-day Adventist Christian. He later studied medicine and practiced in China before fleeing the country in 1949. Finally, he came to the United States to study surgery. Although he planned to return to Asia, a chain of events brought him to eastern Kentucky.

Known as the "Little Chinese Hillbilly," Chu worked from a clinic and traveled by jeep to make house calls. He once said the mountain people often called for him, not because they were sick, but because they had never seen a "Chinaman."

Another Adventist physician, Dr. Ira Wheeler, joined the Oneida Mountain Hospital in 1961 when the charge for an office visit was three dollars and a hospital room was only seven dollars a day. Wheeler worked alone for three months—spending the first few nights at the hospital and sleeping on an examination table because he had no telephone at home in the event of an emergency.

Herb Davis was appointed administrator in 1963, and over the next 11 years he led the hospital through a major relocation and construction project. When he and his wife Pat drove up to the

Oneida Mountain Hospital for the first time, they were tempted to return to their previous jobs at the Florida Sanitarium and Hospital in Orlando.

"We came to see it, so let's go in," Pat finally said.

The three-story, brick structure measuring approximately 50 feet by 55 feet housed patient beds, a clinic, laundry, physical therapy, lab, X-ray, housekeeping, dietary, a pharmacy, medical records, a business office, and an operating/delivery room. Three toilets, one on each floor, served the entire building. Patients crowded the narrow hallways waiting to see doctors.

Davis soon learned that hallways filled with patients did not translate into a healthy bottom line. When he arrived on the job, the hospital had $5,000 in operating capital and a payday coming. He learned that doctors admitted few patients because they did not have money to pay their bills. Davis told the doctors to admit patients and let him worry about collecting payments—a plan that proved successful.

The nursing staff consisted of two registered nurses and three licensed practical nurses. About two months after Davis' arrival, the state notified him that he must provide 24-hour coverage by registered nurses in order to remain in the Kentucky medical assistance program, which represented about 60 percent of the hospital's income. Davis recruited nurses from other Adventist hospitals as far away as Hinsdale, Illinois, and Portland, Oregon. Many came from Madison College near Nashville—a source on which he relied for several years.

In time the hospital's bottom line began to improve, thanks to various philanthropic foundations, changes in reimbursement rates, and improved management. With the introduction of Medicare, admissions increased dramatically. At times the 22-bed hospital had 49 patients. While the government program brought increased census, it also brought a host of regulations and requirements, many of which the old hospital facility could not meet. Davis knew the place could never withstand a fire. Clearly, Clay County needed a new hospital.

After scouting around, Chu, Wheeler, and Davis located a suitable property. They selected an architectural firm, had preliminary plans drawn, and the community began an ambitious fundraising campaign. Things seemed to be on schedule when, without any explanation, the state department of health rejected the project site. Davis and the doctors selected a second site, and the state rejected that one, too. This was one of many hurdles to jump before Clay County would get a new hospital.

Finally, local farmer Saul Goins agreed to sell part of his property for the project. He was not actually interested in selling his farm, but he did so because he wanted a hospital. As far as Davis knew, the state department of health never officially inspected this site, and plans to build got underway.

The building site required a bridge for access from the road, but the highway department requested proof that Davis had funding for the hospital before it committed to building a bridge. This presented another problem for Davis because he had no money.

"All I can offer is my word and my faith in the project," Davis told Jimmy Lucas at the state highway department office.

Lucas paused. "Well, Davis, if that's all you've got, that's all you've got," he said.

Davis never knew what Lucas told his superiors at the state office, but within a short time, construction of the bridge had begun.

Time after time, Davis was reminded of the Lord's provision in building Memorial Hospital. One night he could not sleep as he thought about the various tasks requiring his attention. He made a mental note that the 10-foot ravine separating the road and the hospital must be filled immediately and promised to take care of the matter in the morning. When he arrived at work the next day, the ravine was filled.

"I had made no arrangements for the fill, no discussion had taken place. To this day, I have no knowledge of who filled it or paid for it," he said.

Another instance of divine provision took place regarding government funding. Davis sat on a state committee that recommended projects for Appalachian 202 funding, which provided health care services in poverty-stricken areas. While Clay County was not eligible for this funding, he saw an opportunity to push the limits of the legislation requirements when members of the committee were invited to submit proposals for possible projects.

Davis showed up at a committee meeting with an armload of packets about the plans for the new Memorial Hospital. He included preliminary drawings, cost estimates, project descriptions, and a full-color brochure. He walked around the table placing a packet before each committee member. Although one man firmly objected, Davis continued.

"Mr. Chairman, I worked as a door-to-door salesman when I was younger, and never once did a man come to my door to buy my product. I always had to take it to him," he said. "This committee has to begin somewhere. Use my proposal as a guinea pig if you wish, but don't throw it out."

"This man is endeavoring to hog up the total project. Give us some time and we can drum up a project also," pleaded another committee member.

Davis could not contain himself. "Mr. Chairman, if this gentleman has sat here with us for these past several months and he still needs time to drum up a project, it is evident that he doesn't have much need."

It was a long process, but in the end, Memorial Hospital received approval for Appalachian 202 funds, which automatically meant approval for Hill-Burton funds. Together, these sources covered 80 percent of the construction costs for the new hospital. The community raised the remaining 20 percent.

Of all the people in the community who helped build Memorial Hospital, one name stands above the rest. Marie Langdon and her husband Roy operated the Kozy Motel in Manchester. On one of Mr. Langdon's doctor visits, he learned that the hospital's request for a federal grant had been turned down due to the lack of collateral and community action. He volunteered his wife to lead a community campaign.

Marie Langdon admitted she had always wanted to do something for the hospital, but raising $200,000 was considerably more than she had in mind. Undaunted, she converted her biscuit board into a desk and started writing fundraising letters as well as articles for the local *Manchester Enterprise*. She eventually wrote 4,000 personal letters—all by hand—on behalf of the new hospital. It took six weeks to raise the first $1,000, and Marie remembered the first gift well—five well-worn dollar bills delivered in a small paper bag by a widow who read one of her newspaper articles.

Throughout the campaign, Mrs. Langdon insisted that every dollar counted. She organized box suppers, quilt and craft sales, and a variety of contests. There were teen dances, school band concerts, raffles, gifts from the Future Farmers of America and 4-H Club members, and a four-and-one-half-hour closed-circuit telethon originating from the basement of the Manchester Presbyterian Church.

The Langdons kept a goal board on display at the Kozy Motel and were not above asking guests to contribute to the cause. On one occasion, Mrs. Langdon noticed a likeness of Colonel Harland Sanders on a guest's pen when he signed his name. She inquired and learned that indeed the image on the pen was the famous gentleman of Kentucky Fried Chicken fame. The man assured her he would tell the Colonel about the hospital, and he gave her the pen, which was imprinted with the company's address.

She wrote the Colonel, asking for a donation by July 15, her birthday. Two days before her birthday, Colonel Sanders' secretary called to offer his apology for not sending a donation. Marie was disappointed, but not for long. The Colonel himself called on her birthday and promised $1,500—enough to furnish a patient room.

The story of Aunt Sophia's quilt is another illustration of the grassroots effort that brought the new hospital in Manchester to a reality. Mrs. Langdon's 83-year-old Aunt Sophia Philpot, a former Clay County resident, wrote her niece a letter.

"I love Kentucky, Clay County, and especially Manchester," she said. "I've prayed many times that someday a hospital would be built there…I don't have money to donate…I'm sending you a quilt top…."

When the quilt top arrived, Mrs. Langdon took it to the Bull Skin Quilters in Oneida to be hand-quilted. Then she ran an article in the *Enterprise* asking for donations. She explained that the name of each person who contributed five dollars or more would be placed in a sealed coffee can. When donations reached $1,000, a name would be drawn to determine the winner of the quilt top.

Donations were slightly under goal when Langdon decided to make some personal visits. She first stopped to see Aunt Sophia's sister and brother-in-law, Uncle Jake and Aunt Lucy Sandlin, who were relaxing in the swing on their front porch when she arrived. After listening to her story, Uncle Jake gave her 25 dollars.

"We've already given to the hospital, but I'll give on Sophia's quilt," he said.

Langdon still needed 50 dollars when she reached Uncle Holt Finley's place. When she told him about the quilt and drawing, he called his wife.

One night he could not sleep as he thought about the various tasks requiring his attention. He made a mental note that the 10-foot ravine separating the road and the hospital must be filled immediately and promised to take care of the matter in the morning. When he arrived at work the next day, the ravine was filled.

"Dahlia, get my checkbook and write Marie a check. It is getting late and she wants to go home."

The next morning she took the quilt and the coffee can to Hatcher's Kentucky Food Store where Tommy Hatcher hosted his radio program.

"Folks, here comes Marie Langdon with a quilt under her arm," he announced when he saw her coming. "Let's see what she has on her mind."

When she said she wanted to hold a drawing, Hatcher took the can, shook it several times, and cut the tape on the lid. Pauline Philpot Massey, the store cashier, pulled the name from the can and announced the winner. It was Uncle Jake. Langdon and James Nolan from the *Manchester Enterprise* delivered the quilt and took a picture for the newspaper.

It took many gifts—large ones, small ones, and some given at great personal sacrifice—and yards and yards of political red tape before the 63-bed Memorial Hospital finally opened. The stories of how this hospital came into being illustrate the way the Adventist church and a local community can work together to meet the health care needs of a medically underserved area. They are stories of faith, dedication, determination, and old-fashioned resourcefulness. The people who built Manchester Memorial Hospital clearly understood that every dollar counts.

SOURCES

Allen, Jane, "Heritage of Caring: The Story of Memorial Hospital's Beginning," 1996.

Langdon, Marie, *My True Life and Story and Testimony*, North Newton, Kansas: Mennonite Press, Inc., 1983.

Ogle, Mary S., *China Nurse: The Life Story of Elisabeth Redelstein*, Mountain View, California: Pacific Press Publishing Association, 1974.

A Dentist's Memorial to His Parents

Texas Health Huguley Hospital: Fort Worth, Texas | Founded 1977

Dr. Herbert Taylor Huguley, a Dallas dentist, attended a camp meeting in 1966 where he sat through a long presentation on the church's plans for the Lone Star State. He listened with interest as one speaker shared his dream to build a major health care facility to serve as the flagship for several small Adventist hospitals in Texas. It would also function as a clinical site for nursing students attending the church's college in Keene. After the presentation, Huguley approached

Ben Leach, then president of the Southwestern Union Conference of Seventh-day Adventists.

"One of these days I'm going to surprise you," he told Leach.

Huguley was considered to be "a man of independent means, very generous with the church and with those he loved." He had served as a lieutenant commander in the U.S. Navy during World War II and afterwards had made some successful investments. He was the kind of person who provided free dental services to needy patients. He never married, and his only sister had died in an auto accident, leaving him the sole heir to a valuable family estate.

About a week after the camp meeting, Huguley prepared a handwritten will, leaving most of his estate to the Seventh-day Adventist Church to build a hospital in memory of his parents. Only 10 months later he died at age 69. At that time the value of the property he willed to the church approached $4 million.

After learning of the Adventists' plan to build a hospital in the area, public officials and business leaders in nearby Fort Worth encouraged the church to look in their direction. A hospital would help attract new business, they reasoned. Paul Pewitt, a philanthropist with oil and ranching interests, donated 25 acres for the project and sold the church an additional 25 acres for $50,000, providing a total of 50 acres for the hospital site. Unlike other major hospitals in the area, which were located in the city limits, Huguley Hospital would be built on a prairie site along Interstate 35W. Later, the Texas Electric Service Company purchased five of the 50 acres for $65,000— $15,000 more than the initial cost of all 50.

At least one person in the Fort Worth Chamber of Commerce had some previous experience with Adventist hospitals. Bill Shelton, executive vice president, told Milton Murray, the denominational fundraising consultant, that his mother had been a patient at Hinsdale Hospital near Chicago.

"She loved the hospital, she loved the people there, and when Shelton had visited her, he was highly impressed with the way it was run," Murray reported.

The Chamber of Commerce strongly supported the hospital's campaign to raise more than $3.25 million. The involvement of Alcon Laboratories, one of the largest companies in the area and one of the closest to the hospital site, was expected to help generate support from other companies.

In studying the situation and applying the appropriate fundraising formulas, Murray estimated that Alcon would give them approximately $50,000. Certainly he was not prepared when the company came through with a donation of only $500. He immediately went to William Conner, chairman and a founder of Alcon and member of the campaign committee. Conner, who was familiar with Adventist hospitals, explained that Alcon did not give to brick-and-mortar projects.

Murray knew this company's participation was absolutely essential to the success of the fundraising campaign in Fort Worth, and he had to figure out some way to substantially involve the organization. Finally, he came up with the idea of asking Alcon to support a health education program. Conner liked the idea. Murray prepared another proposal, Alcon agreed to it, and the capital campaign was off to a good start.

Huguley has had a close relationship with local businesses throughout its history, beginning with the Fort Worth Leadership Committee organized before the hospital was built. Members included representatives from Alcon, Continental National Bank, Central Bank and Trust, Texas Electric Service, and First National Bank of Fort Worth, in addition to legal firms and area businesses. When it came to fundraising, $3.25 million came from such corporations and foundations as Texas Electric Service Company, The Tandy Corporation, Southwestern Bell Telephone Company, Lone Star Gas Company, Alcon, Mrs. Baird's Bakery, Bell Helicopter, General Dynamics, Amon

G. Carter Foundation, and the Maybe, Davidson, and Hearst foundations.

Construction of the $16 million, 125-bed facility began in 1974. According to the hospital's first president, Bill Wiist, construction went pretty much as planned. One of the biggest problems was runaway inflation, which made it difficult for builders to get firm prices on supplies. Nevertheless, the new hospital—a contemporary structure of white split block built on a Texas prairie—opened in early 1977, only two months behind schedule and $700,000 under budget.

Huguley was considered to be "a man of independent means, very generous with the church and with those he loved." He had served as a lieutenant commander in the U.S. Navy during World War II and afterwards had made some successful investments. He was the kind of person who provided free dental services to needy patients.

In keeping with its early agreement with Alcon, Huguley made a major commitment to health education and wellness with the opening of The Health Fitness Center in 1985. Funds to build the 41,000 square-foot facility came from a $3 million community campaign and a $1.5 million grant from the Ella C. McFadden Charitable Trust. To this day, health education and fitness programs remain integral to Huguley Hospital's mission.

Adventist Health System formed a joint venture in 2012 with Texas Health Resources to share governance of the hospital. The facility's name was changed to Texas Health Huguley Hospital Fort Worth South. Adventist Health System continues to manage daily operations of the facility.

SOURCES

"Huguley Hospital Celebrates 10th Anniversary," *Southwestern Union Record*, February 27, 1987.

Knott, Ronald Alan, *The Makings of a Philanthropic Fundraiser*, San Francisco, California: Jossey-Bass Publishers, 1992.

Schaffer, Richard A., *Legacy: Daring to Care*, Loma Linda, California: Legacy Publishing Association, 1995.

Whitehead, Mary, "Huguley Hospital—The Beginnings," 1991.

WHY SEVENTH-DAY ADVENTIST HOSPITALS?

By George Nelson*

"Our medical institutions are established to relieve the sick and the afflicted, to awaken a spirit of inquiry, to disseminate light, and to advance reform." – Ellen G. White

To introduce this presentation I wish to borrow from my friend, the late, great Harley Rice; poet, philosopher, world traveler, author. In the field of leadership, especially health care administration, he was a giant.

"The medical ministry of the church," he once wrote, "is made up of ideas, people, and things. The things—bricks and mortar, equipment, machinery—are probably the least important of the three, though things are indispensable. An idea or a conviction without people is but an academic profundity. It requires people to give ideas and convictions the breath of life. The medical ministry of the church finds its fulfillment only through the lives of people. The joy of contributing to the success of the church in its great ministry of salvation; the quiet satisfaction at the end of the day of having done good and faithful work to lessen the sorrows of mankind; the happiness of feeling that one is involved in a joint endeavor with the Great Physician and in being lost in something bigger than oneself is beyond price....

"By its very nature, the contact is made when people are sick and often in pain. These are times when they are prone to be thinking about the serious values of life. In times of acute

illness, when one is laid low, (s)he may realize that life is brief at best. Such an awareness causes one to think about the great hereafter and to measure life by its values which are truer than money or possessions. Thus, the medical ministry of the church in its widest application—and that includes every person who helps to make up the Adventist medical ministry—tends to reach people in their more serious moments, when the door of the heart is more likely to be ajar. At the bedside in the quiet of evening one can say, 'How long we live is not all that counts. How well we live is also important. God promises a life beyond the brevity of our years here….'

"Adventist medical ministry is unique only when it combines science with compassion, competence with love, and skill with understanding and sympathy. When these are combined, the world takes notice….

"Christ's love and sympathy, His understanding, compassion and healing spoke for itself, and multitudes heard and followed. In the world today there is still that desperate need for love, for sympathy, for understanding, for compassion. Hearts ache and tears flow for lack of these elements as much as for causes born of physical pain. These needs are as old as history and date back to the first funeral service on earth and to the first crop of thistles that ever cast their seed on tear-spattered sod."

In denominational publications many references are made to our medical institutions and their purposes. I think, however, that the substance of all the counsels is well stated in a single sentence: 'Our medical institutions are established to relieve the sick and the afflicted, to awaken a spirit of inquiry, to disseminate light, and to advance reform.'

What a marvelous statement! In our medical institutions we should put forth strong endeavor to carry out these principles. In order to do this by way of an organization, it is necessary that all those who share in the program understand its purpose, for the spirit of an institution is found not only in its physical facilities but in the attitudes, the personalities, the will and the dedication of its people.

The first purpose is very clear—to relieve the sick and the afflicted. The second—to awaken a spirit of inquiry, puzzled me a little at first, but the more I have thought about it over the years, the more value and wisdom I see in it. It is a stimulus to create an atmosphere that is so appealing, so striking, so different, that people will not at first understand it, but will be impressed by it. This purpose is achieved, not so much by what is said as by what is done. Though it is important to know what to say, it is very important to know what not to say. What a richness there might be to our influence if all could be engulfed in an atmosphere of Christian love and dignity, and in that pervading atmosphere work with quiet, cheerful, dignified efficiency. In such circumstances our words, our actions, our work, our attitudes and the atmosphere surrounding us may cause others to ask: 'What causes the influence I am experiencing here?' 'What is different about this place?' 'Why is Saturday a quiet day here?' 'Why do you recommend that I modify my diet?' Perhaps some might even be inclined to ask, 'What shall I do to be saved?' Maybe we need to ask ourselves that last question. When John the Baptist was preaching in the desert near Jerusalem, some of the people who heard him asked, 'What shall we do to be saved?' John answered, 'He that hath two coats, let him impart to him that hath none; and he that hath meat, let him do likewise.' In other words, be generous.

Others who asked that same questions were the publicans, the tax gatherers who had bought the right to exact as much as possible from the people in that district, retaining any surplus they might collect as their own property. John's response to these men was clear, honest, and forthright. 'Exact no more than that which is appointed you.' In other words, be honest and fair.

Then came the soldiers—we are all soldiers of the cross—and maybe John's answer to their question about what they should do to be saved has a special application to us. His reply to them was, 'Do violence to no man, neither accuse any falsely; and be content with your wages.' This is all! It was just as simple as that.

In modern English, be kind, stop criticizing, and be content. Even more tersely said, 'Stop fussing and complaining about others, and be satisfied.' If we do just that, it is likely that more and more will ask us, 'What shall I do to be saved?'

Thirdly, the hospital and its people should disseminate light. When a spirit of inquiry has been awakened in the minds of those who see or receive the ministry of healing, it should be possible to answer their questions in a way that will properly cause light to shine where darkness existed.

An area in which the hospital must disseminate light is in teaching the principles of healthful living. This is done by individual example and advice, by classes of instruction for personnel, and by public programs conducted by trained health workers from many sections of the hospital complex..."

The fourth great purpose is to advance reform. What is reform? It is to change into a new form, to amend, to improve, to change. It is the opposite of stagnation. In the sense in which it is used here, it means to retain what is good from the past, and accept what is proved to be good from the new. This is not counsel that applies to a given time and situation. It is living instruction. It means the same today that it meant 75 years ago. It means advance! Move forward! Don't stand still! Advance change!

...I close with a comment about a vital part of our health ministry and the final result we all strive for. It is the hope that the unpublicized, personal witness of the many individuals involved in bringing healing to the sick, combined with the public ministry of the word and song and service, will ultimately result in recognizing familiar but unexpected faces and hearing familiar but unexpected voices joining in the great song described in the colorful words of Revelation 15:3, 4.

---

* Reprinted by permission, George Nelson, *The Kettering Medical Center: Recollections and Reflections on the Early Years*, 1996.

CHRONOLOGY

The following list of sanitariums and hospitals are presently or were in the past operated by the Seventh-day Adventist church and/or one of the Adventist led health systems. Jane Allen Quevedo compiled this list while researching information for her book, *A Thousand Miracles Every Day*, from which this book derived its stories. In some cases the facilities did not operate continuously, and several of the dates are approximate. While not 100 percent complete, the list provides a fair record of the global presence of Adventist hospitals from 1866 to 2016.

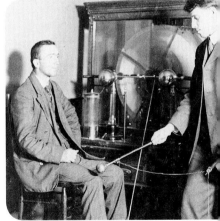

YEAR(s)	HOSPITAL
1866-1876	Western Health Reform Institute
1876-1933	Battle Creek Sanitarium, Battle Creek, Michigan
1878	St. Helena Hospital, Deer Park, California
1888-1912	Mount Vernon Sanitarium, Mount Vernon, Ohio
1893-1989	Boulder Memorial Hospital, Boulder, Colorado
1893-1905	Chicago Sanitarium, Chicago, Illinois
1893	Portland Adventist Medical Center, Portland, Oregon
1894-1907	Guadalajara Sanitarium, Mexico
1895-1910	American Medical Missionary College, Battle Creek, Michigan
1895	Lake Geneva Sanitarium, Switzerland
1895-1920	Nebraska Sanitarium, Lincoln, Nebraska
1895-1906	Samoa Sanitarium, Samoa
1897-1905	Claremont Sanitarium, South Africa
1898-1992	Skodsborg Sanitarium, Denmark
1899-1903	Avondale Health Retreat, Australia
1899-1999	Boston Regional, Stoneham, Massachusetts
1899-1943	Iowa Sanitarium, Nevada, Iowa
1899	Walla Walla General Hospital, Walla Walla, Washington
1900-1907	Calcutta Sanitarium, India
1900-1912	Christchurch Sanitarium, New Zealand
1900-1906	Little Rock Sanitarium, Little Rock, Arkansas
1901-1924	Friedensau Sanitarium, Germany

1902-1907	Buffalo Sanitarium, Buffalo, New York
1902-1928	Kansas Sanitarium and Hospital, Wichita, Kansas
1902-1907	Keene Sanitarium (Lone Star Sanitarium), Keene, Texas
1902-1922	Madison Sanitarium, Madison, Wisconsin
1902-1924	Tri-City Sanitarium, Moline, Illinois
1903-1906	Arizona Sanitarium, Phoenix, Arizona
1903	Atlanta Sanitarium, Atlanta, Georgia
1903-1949	Dr. Harry Miller's arrival marks the beginning of Adventist sanitariums and clinics in China. According to the 1951 Yearbook, more than a dozen facilities were operating in 1949.
1903-1908	Knowlton Sanitarium, Canada
1903	Sydney Adventist Hospital, Australia
1904-1934	Cape Sanitarium, South Africa
1904-1915	Graysville Sanitarium and Hospital, Graysville, Tennessee
1904-2007	Paradise Valley Hospital, National City, California
1904	Philadelphia Sanitarium, Philadelphia, Pennsylvania
1905	Glendale Adventist Medical Center, Glendale, California
1905-1980's	Gopalganj Hospital, Bangladesh
1905	Loma Linda University Health, Loma Linda, California
1905	Adventist Medical Center Hinsdale, Hinsdale, Illinois
1905-1997	Nyhyttan Health and Rehabilitation Center, Sweden
1906-1932	Wabash Valley Sanitarium, Lafayette, Indiana
1907-1913	Black River Sanitarium, Watertown, New York
1907-2006	Tennessee Christian Medical Center Portland, Portland, Tennessee

1907	Washington Adventist Hospital, Takoma Park, Maryland
1908-1919	Adelaide Sanitarium, Australia
1908	Florida Hospital, Orlando, Florida
1908	Malamulo Hospital, Malawi
1908-1910	Mussoorie Sanitarium, India
1908-1927	Nebraska Branch Sanitarium, Hastings, Nebraska
1908	River Plate Sanitarium and Hospital, Argentina
1908-WW II	Soonan Hospital, Korea
1908-2005	Tennessee Christian Medical Center, Madison, Tennessee
1909-1912	Rock City Sanitarium, Nashville, Tennessee
1910-1923	Huntsville Sanitarium, Huntsville, Alabama
1910	Park Ridge Health, Fletcher, North Carolina
1910-2000	Warburton Adventist Hospital, Australia
1912-1968	Stanboroughs Nursing and Maternity Home, England
1913	White Memorial Medical Center, Los Angeles, California
1914-1992	Hadley Memorial Hospital, Washington, D.C.
1914-1988	Scott Memorial Hospital, Lawrenceburg, Tennessee
1915-1949	Nanning Seventh-day Adventist Hospital, Kwangsi, China
1915	Simla Sanitarium and Hospital, India
1916-1968	Chuharkana Hospital Dispensary, Pakistan
1916-1947	Yencheng Sanitarium, China
1917-1925	Bethel Sanitarium, Canada
1918-1923	Douglasville Sanitarium, Douglasville, Georgia
1918-1949	Shanghai Medical Center, China

CHRONOLOGY

1920	Berlin Hospital, Germany
1920	El Reposo Sanitarium, Florence, Alabama
1920-1957	Pisgah Sanitarium and Hospital, Candler, North Carolina
1921	Kanye Hospital, Botswana
1921-1979	Rest Haven Hospital, Canada
1922	Juliaca Adventist Clinic, Peru
1924	Penang Adventist Hospital, Malaysia
1925	Giffard Memorial Hospital, India
1925	Kendu Adventist Hospital, Kenya
1925-WW II	Narsapur Seventh-day Adventist Mission Hospital, India
1925	Pewee Valley Sanitarium, near Louisville, Kentucky
1926	Hultafors Health Centre, Sweden
1927-1958	Georgia Sanitarium, Atlanta, Georgia
1927	Mwami Adventist Hospital, Zambia
1927-1983	Riverside Sanitarium and Hospital, Nashville, Tennessee
1927	Songa Adventist Hospital, Democratic Republic of Congo
1928-1975	Bongo Mission Hospital, Angola
1928-1977	Sonnenhof Sanitarium, Germany
1928	Takoma Regional Hospital, Greeneville, Tennessee
1929	Manila Sanitarium and Hospital, Philippines
1929-1936	Taffari Makonnen Hospital, Ethiopia
1929	Tokyo Adventist Hospital, Japan
1930	Porter Adventist Hospital, Denver, Colorado
1930-1939	Sultanbad Hospital, Iran

1931	Mugonero Hospital, Rwanda
1932-1976	Empress Zauditu Memorial Adventist Hospital, Ethiopia
1934-1975	Haile Selassie I Hospital, Ethiopia
1934-1991	Pine Forest Sanitarium and Hospital, Gilbertown, Alabama
1935	Lanchow Sanitarium, China
1935	Seoul Adventist Hospital, Korea
1936-1978	Kwailibesi Hospital, Solomon Islands
1936-1959	Nokuphila Hospital, South Africa
1936	Surat Hospital, India
1936-1949	Wuhan Sanitarium, China
1937	Bangkok Adventist Hospital, Thailand
1937-1995	Fuller Memorial Hospital, South Attleboro, Massachusetts
1937-1978	Kukudu Hospital (Amyes Memorial Hospital), Solomon Islands
1937-1945	Maun Medical Mission Hospital, Zambesi
1939-1942	Good View Clinic, Brazil
1940	Little Creek Sanitarium, Knoxville, Tennessee
1940	Phuket Adventist Hospital, Thailand
1942	Sao Paulo Adventist Hospital, Brazil
1942	Wildwood Sanitarium, Wildwood, Georgia
1943	Hopeaniemi Health and Rehabilitation Center, Finland
1944	Seventh-day Adventist Hospital Ile-Ife, Nigeria
1945	Andrews Memorial Hospital, Jamaica, West Indies
1946-1959	Dar Es-Salaam Hospital, aka The House of Peace Hospital, Iraq
1946	Miraflores Adventist Clinic, Peru

1946	Montemorelos University Hospital, Mexico
1946	Skogli Health and Rehabilitation Center, Norway
1947-1992	Ardmore Adventist Hospital, Ardmore, Oklahoma
1947-1964	Forsyth Memorial Sanitarium and Hospital, Tallahassee, Florida
1947	Gimbie Hospital, Ethiopia
1947	Jengre Seventh-day Adventist Hospital, Nigeria
1947-1965	Rangoon Adventist Hospital, Myanmar (Burma)
1948	Community Hospital of Seventh-day Adventists, Trinidad, West Indies
1948	Florida Hospital Heartland Medical Center, Sebring, Florida (formerly Walker Memorial Hospital, Avon Park)
1948-1980	Nicaragua Adventist Hospital, Nicaragua
1948	Silvestre Adventist Hospital, Brazil
1948-1995	Youngberg Memorial Adventist Hospital
1949	Heri Adventist Hospital, Tanzania
1949	Ranchi Adventist Hospital, India
1950	Bandung Adventist Hospital, Java, Indonesia
1950	Feather River Hospital, Paradise, California
1950	Ishaka Adventist Hospital, Uganda
1950	Karachi Adventist Hospital, Pakistan
1950	Penfigo Adventist Hospital, Brazil
1950-1982	Togoba Hospital, New Guinea
1951	Maluti Adventist Hospital, South Africa
1951	Pusan Adventist Hospital, Korea
1952	Mindanao Sanitarium and Hospital, Philippines

1952	North Norway Rehabilitation Center, Norway
1953	Adventist Medical Center, Okinawa, Japan
1953	Belem Adventist Hospital, Brazil
1954	Bella Vista Hospital, Puerto Rico
1954	Davis Memorial Clinic and Hospital, Guyana
1954-1988	Haad Yai Mission Hospital, Thailand
1954-1964	Iceland Summer Sanitarium, Iceland
1954	Koza Adventist Hospital, Republic of Cameroon
1955-1978	Boliu Hospital, Papua New Guinea
1955-1974	Kwahu Hospital, Ghana
1955-1975	Saigon Adventist Hospital, Vietnam
1955-1970	Santa Ana Hospital, Santa Anna, Texas
1955	Taiwan Adventist Hospital, Taiwan
1955	Yuka Adventist Hospital, Zambia
1956-1969	Benghazi Adventist Hospital, Libya
1956	Guam Seventh-day Adventist Clinic, Guam
1956	H. W. Miller Memorial Sanitarium and Hospital, Philippines
1957	Blantyre Adventist Hospital, Malawi
1957-1997	North York Branson Hospital, Canada
1957	Sonora Community Hospital, Sonora, California
1957-1980	Watkins Memorial Hospital, Ellijay, Georgia
1958-1992	Louis Smith Memorial Hospital, Lakeland, Georgia
1958-1980	Menard Hospital, Menard, Texas
1958-1972	Putnam Memorial Hospital, Palatka, Florida

CHRONOLOGY

1959	Asuncion Adventist Sanitarium, Paraguay
1959	Belgrano Adventist Clinic, Argentina
1959	Cagayan Valley Sanitarium and Hospital, Philippines
1959-1992	Parkview Memorial Hospital, Brunswick, Maine
1960	Central Texas Medical Center, San Marcos, Texas
1960	Reading Rehabilitation Hospital, Reading, Pennsylvania
1960	Scheer Memorial Hospital, Nepal
1961	Ana Stahl Adventist Clinic, Peru
1961-1996	Monument Valley Hospital, Mexican Hat, Utah
1961-1970's	New Hebrides SDA Mission Hospital, New Hebrides
1961	Quito Adventist Clinic, Ecuador
1961	Sopas Adventist Hospital, Papua New Guinea
1961-1981	Tempe Community Hospital, Tempe, Arizona
1962	Gingoog Sanitarium and Hospital, Philippines
1962-1985	Memorial Hospital of Bee County, Beeville, Texas
1962	Shawnee Mission Medical Center, Shawnee Mission, Kansas
1963	Castle Medical Center, Kailua, Hawaii
1963	Adventist Medical Center of Hanford, Hanford, California
1964	Kettering Medical Center, Kettering, Ohio
1964	San Joaquin Community Hospital
1964	Tsuen Wan Adventist Hospital, Hong Kong
1965	Bacolod Sanitarium and Hospital, Philippines
1965	Hohenau Adventist Sanitarium, Paraguay
1965-1985	Jay Memorial Hospital, Jay, Oklahoma

1965	Lakeside Adventist Hospital, Sri Lanka
1965	Masanga Leprosy Hospital, Sierra Leone
1965	Simi Valley Hospital and Health Care Services, Simi Valley, California
1966	Atoifi Adventist Hospital, Solomon Islands
1966-1978	Kastiorita Hospital, Papua New Guinea
1966	Loma Linda Adventist Sanitarium, Argentina
1966	Roundelwood (Good Health Association), Scotland
1966	Ruby Nelson Memorial Hospital, India
1969-1986	Marion County Hospital, Jefferson, Texas
1969	Medan Adventist Hospital, Indonesia
1969-1994	Medical Center Hospital, Punta Gorda, Florida
1969	Ottapalam Seventh-day Adventist Hospital, India
1970	Antillean Adventist Hospital, Curacao, Netherlands Antilles
1970	Cave Memorial Clinic and Nursing Home, Barbados,West Indies
1971	Hong Kong Adventist Hospital, Hong Kong
1971	Memorial Hospital, Manchester, Kentucky
1972	Northeast Argentine Sanitarium, Argentina
1973	Calbayog Sanitarium and Hospital, Philippines
1973	Florida Hospital Altamonte, Altamonte Springs, Florida
1973-2016	Hackettstown Community Hospital, Hackettstown, New Jersey
1973	Kobe Adventist Hospital, Japan
1973	Tillamook Regional Medical Center, Tillamook, Oregon
1973	Toole County Adventist Hospital, Shelby, Montana

1974-2000	Auckland Adventist Hospital, New Zealand
1974-2015	Jellico Community Hospital, Jellico, Tennessee (acquired)
1974	Pune Adventist Hospital, India
1974	Valley of the Angels Hospital, Honduras
1975-1991	Anacapa Adventist Hospital, Port Hueneme, California
1975	Florida Hospital Apopka, Apopka, Florida
1975	Southeast Hospital, Mexico
1976	Andapa Adventist Hospital, Madagascar
1976-2014	Emory Adventist Hospital, Smyrna, Georgia
1977	Texas Health Huguley Hospital, Fort Worth, Texas
1978	Adventist Hospital of Haiti, Port-au-Prince, Haiti
1978	Bangalore Adventist Hospital, India
1978	Manaus Adventist Hospital, Brazil
1979	Shady Grove Adventist Hospital, Rockville, Maryland
1979	Ukiah Valley Medical Center, Ukiah, California (acquired)
1980	Chippewa Valley Hospital, Durand, Wisconsin
1980	Sao Roque Adventist Clinic, Brazil
1981	Gordon Hospital, Calhoun, Georgia
1982	Espirito Santo Adventist Hospital, Brazil
1982	Florida Hospital Lake Placid, Lake Placid, Florida
1982	LaPaz Adventist Clinic, Bolivia
1982	Palawan Adventist Hospital, Philippines
1982-1994	Moberly Regional Medical Center, Moberly, Missouri
1982-1987	Reeves County Hospital, Pecos, Texas

1983	Los Angeles Adventist Clinic, Chile
1982-1988	Sierra Vista Hospital, Truth or Consequences, New Mexico
1983	Metroplex Hospital, Killeen, Texas
1983	Venezuela Adventist Hospital, Venezuela
1984	Asamang Seventh-day Adventist Hospital, Ghana
1984	Milton Mattison Memorial Hospital, India
1984	Seventh-day Adventist Hospital and Motherless Babies' Home, Nigeria
1985	Florida Hospital Zephyrhills, Zephyrhills, Florida
1986	Seventh-day Adventist Cooper Hospital, Liberia
1987	Davao Sanitarium and Hospital, Philippines
1987	San Joaquin Community Hospital, Bakersfield, California
1989	Avista Adventist Hospital, Louisville, Colorado
1989	Littleton Adventist Hospital, Littleton, Colorado
1989	Porto Alegre Adventist Clinic, Brazil
1990's	Glei Adventist Eye Hospital, Togo
1990	Bella Vista Polyclinic, Puerto Rico
1990	Dominase Adventist Hospital, Ghana
1990	Florida Hospital East Orlando, Orlando, Florida
1991	Batouri Adventist Hospital, Republic of Cameroon
1991	Rollins-Brook Community Hospital, Lampasas, Texas
1992	Florida Hospital Waterman, Eustis, Florida
1993	Florida Hospital, Kissimmee, Kissimmee, Florida
1993	Florida Hospital Wauchula, Wauchula, Florida
1994	Bandar Lampung Adventist Hospital, Sumatra, Indonesia

CHRONOLOGY

1994	East Bolivia Adventist Clinic, Bolivia
1994	Florida Hospital Fish Memorial, Orange City, Florida
1996	Aizawl Adventist Hospital, India
1996	Thanjavur Adventist Hospital, India
1997	Florida Hospital Celebration Health, Celebration, Florida
1997	GlenOaks Medical Center, Glendale Heights, Illinois
1997	Nova Friburgo Adventist Hospital, Brazil
1998-2002	Southern Medical Center, Puerto Rico
1999	La Grange Memorial Hospital, La Grange, Illinois
2000	Memorial Hospital-Flagler, Bunnell, Florida
2000	Memorial Hospital-Ormond Beach, Ormond Beach, Florida
2000	Memorial Hospital-Peninsula, Ormond Beach, Florida
2000	Florida Hospital DeLand, DeLand, Florida
2000	Winter Park Memorial Hospital, Winter Park, Florida
2002	Florida Hospital Flagler, Palm Coast, Florida
2004	Parker Adventist Hospital, Parker, Colorado
2008	Adventist Bolingbrook Hospital, Bolingbrook, Illinois
2010	Florida Hospital North Pinellas, Tarpon Springs, Florida
2010	Florida Hospital Tampa, Tampa, Florida
2010	Florida Hospital Pepin Heart Institute, Tampa Florida
2010	Florida Hospital Carrollwood, Tampa, Florida
2011	Florida Hospital for Children, Orlando Florida
2012	Florida Hospital Wesley Chapel, Wesley Chapel, Florida
2013	Castle Rock Adventist Hospital, Castle Rock, Colorado

CHRONOLOGY

2014	Murray Medical Center, Chatsworth, Georgia
2016	Florida Hospital for Women, Orlando, Florida
2016	Florida Hospital New Smyrna, New Smyrna Beach, Florida

We invite you to view the complete
selection of titles we publish at:

www.TEACHServices.com

scan with your mobile
device to go directly
to our website

Please write or email us your praises, reactions, or
thoughts about this or any other book we publish at:

TEACH Services, Inc.
P U B L I S H I N G
www.TEACHServices.com ● (800) 367-1844

Info@TEACHServices.com

TEACH Services, Inc., titles may be purchased in bulk for
educational, business, fund-raising, or sales promotional use.
For information, please e-mail:

BulkSales@TEACHServices.com

Finally if you are interested in seeing
your own book in print, please contact us at

publishing@TEACHServices.com

We would be happy to review your manuscript for free.